MARTY DARRACOTT

THE MAN IN THE OFFICE NEXT DOOR

DAVID EDMONDSON

THE MAN IN THE OFFICE NEXT DOOR
by Marty Darracott & David Edmondson

Copyright © 2020 by David Edmondson

ISBN: 978 1 7360233 2 7

Cover Design: Jerry Leaphart

Unless otherwise indicated,
all Scripture quotations are taken from the *New King James Version*, copyright © 1982, Thomas Nelson.
Italics and bold highlights in scriptural passages are for emphasis only.

All rights reserved. No part of this book may be reproduced, distributed, or transmitted in any form or by any means, including electronic, mechanical, photocopying, recording, or any information storage and retrieval system without permission in writing from the author.

All rights reserved.
Printed in the United States of America.

Dedication

OFFICE DOOR 1 (David)

To my forever one, Stephanie Edmondson: You have always believed in and loved me. At this time, it's been 26 years since I first laid my eyes on you for the first time. My prayer is that after many more years together, you will be the last person on earth I lay my eyes on.

OFFICE DOOR 2 (Marty)

To the one who captured my heart: my wife, Paula Jo Darracott. Thank you for your unconditional love. Thank you for modeling excellence, eloquence and elegance 24/7. I love, honor, and adore you. Thank you for giving me two of the greatest gifts of my life, our precious daughters, Madison and Carson.

Acknowledgments

OFFICE DOOR 1

I would like to acknowledge and thank everyone who went through this journey with me and stayed. This process was one of the hardest things to navigate through, but in the end, many of you and I came out on the winning side!

I acknowledge and thank THE MAN IN THE OFFICE NEXT DOOR for forgiving me and helping me walk through this process. I love you and your family with all my heart!

OFFICE DOOR 2

To my two most prized possessions, my treasures, Madison and Carson Darracott. Thank you for modeling such Christ-like character. Thank you for allowing your mother and me to minister the love of God to others all over the world over the last twenty years. Thank you for sharing us with students, parents, and congregations all over the world. Thank you for serving alongside us in school gyms, football stadiums, camps, retreats, and conferences while we do what He put in our hearts to do. I honor you both.

Introduction

People are finicky, easily offended, and territorial, and they get edgy when things don't go just right for them.

Conflict tends to surface in every relationship at some point along the way, even in ministry. Why? Because people are involved.

In the Fall of 2010, division came to a growing and vibrant church in north Georgia. Over the next several years that division morphed into anger, offense, and downright hatred.

This book, *The Man In The Office Next Door*, is a first-hand account of church division told from the very different perspectives of two pastors at the core of the conflict, who, despite a history of great respect and love for each other, and even family ties, allowed conflict to nearly destroy everything they stood for in ministry. In this raw account of the conflict, each party refers to the other as THE MAN IN THE OFFICE NEXT DOOR.

Within these pages, you will read about how one confrontation, left unresolved, ended in years of turmoil. You will get a glimpse of what goes on within most relationships, whether in the context of ministry or secular cooperation, when unresolved offense between coworkers and family members heightens to a level of hatred and separation.

THE MAN IN THE OFFICE NEXT DOOR became disrespectful, dishonoring, bitter, defensive, petty, sensitive, easily-offended, judgmental, arrogant, prideful, spiteful, wounded, restricted, and confined. It was so easy for each party to dislike THE MAN IN THE OFFICE NEXT DOOR, a lot. Then, the closer the men drew to the Lord, the more they realized THE MAN IN THE OFFICE NEXT DOOR is always *ME*!

This book has been birthed through much heartache, extreme emotion, and humble repentance. You will learn the results of unresolved offense, the devastation of un-forgiveness, the leverage of personal influence, and the power of repentance and forgiveness.

Take a journey into the lives of two pastors as they tried to navigate life, family, friendships, and ministry through an extremely turbulent time in their lives. You will read very private and humbling details into each one of the men's experiences as they went from close friends to mortal enemies before ending in nothing short of a miraculous brotherhood.

You owe yourself and your world the lessons learned within the pages of this book! Save yourself years of heartache and isolation as you learn from *The Man In The Office Next Door*.

Table of Contents

Dedication	5
Acknowledgments	7
Introduction	9
First Service. First Contest. First Conflict. (Strengthen the Pillars)	13
Behind Closed Doors (The Harbor for Un-forgiveness)	27
The Café Meeting (Challenge Given– Challenge Accepted)	37
Meeting with The Head Honcho (The Pain of Separation)	49
I Don't Need Him Anyway (Am I my Brother's Keeper?)	59
The Dismissal (The Last Time We Spoke)	73
Family Crisis (You Can't Keep This in the House)	85

The Revival Service (The Power of Repentance and Forgiveness)   93

Like It Never Happened (The Baptism)   117

The Open-Door Policy (Final thoughts)   127

The "Bystanders" (Collateral Damage)   137

Strengthen the Pillars

First Service. First Contest. First Conflict.

OFFICE DOOR 2:

That Sunday was supposed to be like any other in the previous twelve years of my Christian life. Wake up. Get dressed. Go to church. Eat lunch. Come home.

Simple enough. However, on this particular Sunday in 2008, things would be anything but simple.

The senior pastors of my church, my spiritual parents, the couple that had led my wife and me to Christ on December 5, 1993, were transitioning from pastoring at our church, where I served as youth pastor. They had decided to hand the reins of the church over to another one of their spiritual sons. (From this point on, I will refer to him as "THE MAN IN THE OFFICE NEXT DOOR.")

I was totally fine with their decision. This guy could preach the paint off of the walls. He was proven. He was a powerful preacher. This new pastor and his wife also happened to be family, as his wife is my first cousin. Things were great. Life was good.

THE MAN IN THE OFFICE NEXT DOOR was to preach his inaugural message on this particular Sunday. He preached out of Judges 16, one of MY favorite passages to preach from. I've ministered on Samson and Delilah at youth camps, student conferences, fall retreats, and FCA Club Meetings all over the nation. It is one of those messages we preachers receive from the Lord that easily becomes one of our "hip pocket" go-to messages. We can preach it with our eyes closed (Ironically, with NO pun intended. As I say that, I recall the part of the passage where Samson had his eyes gouged out. OUCH!)

The title I had usually given this particular message was, "REMEMBER ME?" As I studied that passage, those two words jumped off the page and began to hover like a drone right in front of me. These are two of the last few words Samson would be able to speak just before his death in Gaza. As powerful and as revelatory as those two words were to me, they suddenly became Samson's epitaph.

I recall THE MAN IN THE OFFICE NEXT DOOR preaching with great passion that Sunday. THE Sunday. His message was entitled "STRENGTHEN THE PILLARS." He shared with us how the enemy would desire nothing more than to get his hands on the church's leadership, the pillars, and bring the house crashing down. He spoke of how Samson knew that the church's pillars were the support structure, the backbone, if you will, of the house. He eloquently communicated several points from the passage about how Samson defeated the Philistines after they had shaved his hair, plucked out his eyes, and assigned him a young boy to lead him around.

It didn't take long at all for me to see the similarities from both his message, "STRENGTHEN THE PILLARS," and the message the Lord had given me, "REMEMBER ME." I sat in amazement as I heard him unpack the message that day. I was tracking right along. That is, until he got near the end of the message and began to compare Samson's last moments on earth with the enemy's desire to attack our lives. He spoke of how the enemy, relating to Samson, eagerly awaits the opportune time to pull down life's pillars all around us, causing debilitating destruction. I hadn't seen it in that light before. I had always preached that passage using the main point that, no matter how far you've gone, no matter how afflicted you've been at the hands of an enemy, it's never too late to cry out to the Lord with a prayer much like Samson's: "REMEMBER ME." And the Lord is faithful to restore His Spirit to us in that instance.

I see now what I could not see then. Two like-minded people can be exposed to the same moment and walk away with two completely different vantage points.

After this powerful Sunday morning message, our church was making preparations to have dinner on the grounds. We were all going outdoors for a great Sunday afternoon in the mild Georgia sun for a time of fun and fellowship and football. It's what we do in the south.

I had scheduled a flag football game for our entire youth ministry and the men of our church. Everything started great. The food and camaraderie were amazing. Some of the guys in our youth group began tossing the football around. I noticed some of the older men stretching. It was almost game time. Game on!

Things could not have been going any better. The weather was nearly perfect. People were smiling, laughing, cheering, egging others on – the fellowship was awesome!

I looked around and thought, "It couldn't get any better than this." I was right. However, things could get worse.

Being the youngest of four kids and growing up playing multiple sports from elementary school through college meant one thing: having a competitive edge was inevitable. It was my intrinsic nature to have the desire to win at anything and everything. It didn't matter if it was a friendly game of ping pong, a game of Horse, or Uno.

I can remember sibling rivalries in everything: who could finish a meal first; who could make it from the car to the front door first; and vice versa, calling "SHOTGUN!" to ensure victory despite the inevitable challenge, "No, I called it first!" A pleasant family walk around the block always ended with us kids fighting to see who could be the first to step on the driveway upon returning home.

The drive to be first at anything – at *everything* – infiltrated my every move. *Second place only meant first loser.*

I remember this flag football game vividly. It was in the second half – you know, when time is dwindling, and both teams do whatever they can do to make sure their team ends up on top. Things quickly went from innocent and silly to serious in a hurry.

It may have been an innocent flag football game at church to some, but for others of us, we realized that this one event would easily lead to one team earning bragging rights for a flag football season (which was one game, one Sunday afternoon, on an annual basis) and the other team having to hear about being second best for an entire year.

What began as a strategic attempt to get our church family outdoors together, spending quality time in Christian fellowship, began to turn toxic quickly. The football field suddenly morphed into a battlefield. Cheering quickly became chipping at each other. Fellowship became a firefight. Touchdowns turned to tempers flaring. Mouths became fiery catapults. Attitudes went south as fast as the time clock.

Tick tock. Tick tock. Tick tock. As both team's scores mounted, the time clock dwindled. The score was tight and pass coverage got even tighter. The game was serious now. We had to remind a couple of guys from each team that FLAG football was not tackle football.

I played quarterback for the youth team. I remember it like it was yesterday (and that's pretty sad seeing that this event happened eleven years ago and it's still etched). Near the end of the game, the score remained close. I remember dropping back and throwing a "Hail Mary" to one of our students only to see him get pushed down as the ball dropped in the end zone.

The other team cheered. My team immediately demanded a pass interference call. The only problem was, there were no referees. We were left to call our own penalties. Surely, as Christians, we would all agree on every call, every time. (Do you sense the sarcasm in my words?)

Remember, it's a Sunday afternoon backyard football game, not a televised ESPN special. Nobody paid admission to get in to watch the game. It was supposed to be a time of great fellowship. It was a "friendly" game of flag football, we thought.

We did not agree on the issue of pass interference.

A meeting ensued at the original line of scrimmage. Both opponents had very vocal representatives sharing their viewpoints openly. That meeting turned into a court of law, and several key players weighed in to state their case. It got heated. Voices got louder, and faces got redder and redder. Team A stood their ground. Team B stood theirs. Nobody won. Everyone lost. It was out of control now. The sidelines got involved as chairs began to fold up. The people had endured all they could stomach. It became a nightmare.

I remember thinking this isn't how I saw this day ending, not the hoped-for outcome. But those thoughts didn't keep me from weighing in as well. I stated my case. THE MAN IN THE OFFICE NEXT DOOR stated his. I adamantly delivered a rebuttal. The two pillars began to shake at their foundations.

Tempers had gotten the best of us. Well, it had unquestionably gotten the best of me. I threw my hands up many times that day. Most of those times were in celebration of the touchdowns my team compiled. But this time, I threw my hands up; it was in frustration. I had had enough. I quit! GAME OVER FOR ME!

I walked off the field with fumes of frustration following me. THE MAN IN THE OFFICE NEXT DOOR and I were at odds – *extreme* odds. My blood began to boil.

I immediately heard what I will call the "whispers of war," voicing their opinions in my mind. Inside, I began to hear things like, "There it is; these are his true colors coming out!" I heard things like, "He's treating you like this, and he is a *pastor*?" "He doesn't love you for you; he merely tolerates you for what you can do for the church he pastors."

These one-liners echoed in my mind. "He hates you! Hate him right back." "There's no rebounding from this." "It's over. If not completely over, at least it will never be the same. Ever!"

SATAN WASTES NO TIME WHEN HE SOWS SEEDS OF DISCORD!

I began to look around the field that Sunday afternoon, and it was as if I began to see everyone in two colors. I saw some in blue and others in gray. I began to hear the voices in my head, and I began to see with my mind's eye: those in blue were for me, and those in gray were for THE MAN IN THE OFFICE NEXT DOOR, and ultimately against me. Men and women surrounded the field that day, either on the field or the sidelines watching, waiting. In my mind, in that exact moment, they were all forced to choose a side. A Civil War was brewing.

The game ended. I could not tell you who won. That point was moot, and it was the least of my worries. There was conflict, now, paralyzing tension. The pillars began to shake that day.

We met the next morning and tried our best to resolve the conflict that had ensued from the *FLAG FOOTBALL GAME* the day before.

As I write this, the mere thought of a conflict birthed in an innocent flag football game – among church members – seems so absurd and embarrassing! We both apologized at the meeting that day. However, the foundation seemed cracked. Things just didn't seem like they could be okay anymore. Caulk and putty wouldn't cut it in this case. We were both hurt and deeply wounded. Our injuries were becoming life-threatening (spiritually speaking).

I'm sure both parties were a bit confused. How could this happen? As pastors and leaders, we were supposed to be messengers of hope, called to model humility and unity, yet here we were at odds – staunch odds – and now divided in every way imaginable.

Looking back now, I realize that the pillars weren't just beginning to shake on that football field that particular Sunday afternoon. That was the precise moment they began to crumble.

Although I felt the immense pain from this devastating body blow, I was secure enough in my faith and in my walk with Christ that I was bound and determined not to tuck my tail and run. My instinct had always been to quit. If dating relationships didn't quit, just break up. If a job didn't pan out, I would resign. Not this time, though.

I chose to stay at the church and not leave as my default setting would suggest. I continued to serve on staff with THE MAN IN THE OFFICE NEXT DOOR. I continued my walk with the Lord. However, that walk began to reveal a slight limp. Now there was external proof of the internal pain. And everyone could see it.

OFFICE DOOR 1:

I will never forget the first service we had as my pastorate began at our church. It was a day I had long-awaited. My pastor and spiritual father had spoken to me years earlier about one day taking over the main campus of the ministry he had begun and built for many years. Being chosen to succeed my mentor in leading the church that he and his wife founded was one of my greatest honors.

The service began like all other services. Our music ministry was powerful, and the song arrangement perfect. The singers were passionate in their worship. The band was spot on, and we had no troubles with the sound system, the lighting, or anything else that tended to arise during big events.

The atmosphere was electric, and you didn't have to be a seasoned minister to preach in that kind of environment, that's for sure.

I remember I had clearly heard from the Lord on what my message was to be. I knew my task was not going to be comfortable, and turning the ship would take time. However, I had one shot to start this journey off on the right foot, and I knew I had the Lord's plan to do just that.

Holy Spirit had shown me how Samson defeated the Philistines after they had shaved his hair, plucked out his eyes, and assigned him a young boy to lead him around. The Bible tells us that hundreds and hundreds of Philistines were on the roof of a building looking down on Samson and making fun of him because they had stripped him of his strength.

Just before Samson prayed to the Lord to give him the power to destroy the Philistines and avenge him of his greatest enemy one last time, he requested the lad that was leading him around. He asked the lad to let him feel the pillars of the house. He said, just let me lean on the pillars holding up the house.

My message that service was "Strengthen the Pillars." I told the congregation how the enemy wants to put his hands on the pillars, the church's leaders. If he could get to them, he could bring the whole house down.

You see, Samson knew if he could bring down the main pillars of the structure, then the whole place would crumble. Of course, we know Samson was able to do just that. He broke the pillars, and the entire structure fell, killing all those who depended on it to remain standing.

After what I felt was an unbelievable first service, we all went out to play flag football. THE MAN IN THE OFFICE NEXT DOOR had scheduled an outing for our youth group to play flag football and celebrate our new beginning together. This was not unusual seeing that THE MAN IN THE OFFICE NEXT DOOR was our youth pastor, and we had events like this very often.

Everything was going amazingly well. Several dozen youths were playing and having fun. Young adults came to watch and cheer, and some even stretched the limitations of their ages by playing in the football games.

Children were playing games, and young couples were walking in the grass with their babies. Many people were on the sidelines, cheering on their friends and family. We were all having a great time. THE MAN IN THE OFFICE NEXT DOOR was quarterbacking his team, and they were putting a hurting on the opposing team. There was laughter, excitement, unity, joy, and all the other emotions that come with the new life we had all just set out on together.

That was, until the conflict.

I decided, against my better judgment, to go out onto the field and try my hand at a little football myself. It seemed everyone was having such a good time, and after all, I was a quarterback in high school, not too many moons earlier in life. I saw this as an opportunity for me to build relationships with the people I was not directly in charge of shepherding.

Everyone playing was having a great time, joking back and forth, giving each other the typical playful cut downs that come with playing sports. So I wanted to join in. THE MAN IN THE OFFICE NEXT DOOR was laughing, making jokes, challenging the other team's players, so I thought I would join the other team and lead them to a comeback victory.

Well, things could not have gone worse. I jumped on to the field and played quarterback for the other team. I began court-jesting with THE MAN IN THE OFFICE NEXT DOOR. I began to joke with him, challenge him, and poke a little fun at him. In all sincerity, I was just trying to be part of the game and participate in the fun I noticed everyone else was having. That was, until I must have said the wrong thing!

I don't remember what it was that I said. I am sure it was not nice, uplifting, or even appropriate, but suddenly, THE MAN IN THE OFFICE NEXT DOOR stopped playing and just walked off the field. Everyone began to ask him to come back and play. I even pushed the envelope a little bit and asked him to come back, although my comments had a negative and slighting tone.

THE MAN IN THE OFFICE NEXT DOOR would not respond and just walked off, explaining that he didn't want to play. There was conflict; trouble was brewing. Discord was in the air, as the enemy had placed his hands on the pillars and pushed. Our response was to crumble under pressure.

I played a few minutes longer, but I knew I had messed up. I went to the sidelines. As soon as I left the game, THE MAN IN THE OFFICE NEXT DOOR began to play again. Some friends on the sidelines told me to stop the game and apologize and make things right. But I was crumbling. The enemy's hands were on me, and I was cracking – and I didn't even know it.

I felt like I had done nothing wrong. I felt like it was all THE MAN IN THE OFFICE NEXT DOOR's fault. He was just acting like a baby and couldn't take the pressure. In reality, we were both on trial, and we were both under conviction for crumbling under the weight of what was happening in the spirit.

That day was the beginning – not of building an incredible ministry team – but the beginning of the end of a dynamic duo. See, THE MAN IN THE OFFICE NEXT DOOR and I were supposed to be the Dream Team. We were both so gifted to lead others and inspire people to love Jesus, chase their dreams, and achieve greatness in their lives. However, that day I let the enemy feel the pillars.

Yes, as any good leader should, I met with THE MAN IN THE OFFICE NEXT DOOR the next morning to discuss the events that took place. Even though we both "said" we were sorry, the damage to the foundation was not healed. The apologies were heard and spoken in the natural realm but never really addressed in the spiritual realm.

The Bible teaches that out of the heart flows the issues of life. My heart had taken a slow turn against THE MAN IN THE OFFICE NEXT DOOR, and I didn't even know it. The man I was supposed to lead, love, and encourage slowly became my enemy in my heart, and I had no idea. THE MAN IN THE OFFICE NEXT DOOR was hurting. He was confused. He needed guidance on handling his emotions, but I was too caught up in my feelings to realize this great opportunity I had to be the great leader I challenged other people to be.

The first service, the first contest, and the first conflict ended up being the first of many more times THE MAN IN THE OFFICE NEXT DOOR, and I would collapse under the weight of our pain and misunderstandings.

LESSON LEARNED: Many times, the enemy doesn't wait for us to get grounded in a situation before the attack comes. This is why we must always be on guard. Jesus taught a parable found in Matthew chapter 13. In the parable, Jesus shows us that, as once the "seed," or the Word of God, is planted into our lives the enemy, immediately comes to steal the Word. Our enemy never sleeps! Stay vigilant and always protect yourself from the sudden attacks.

Behind Closed Doors

The Harbor for Unforgiveness

OFFICE DOOR 1:

Over the next several months, THE MAN IN THE OFFICE NEXT DOOR and I would continue to distance ourselves from each other – well, as much as we could, seeing as how our relationship was multifaceted. THE MAN IN THE OFFICE NEXT DOOR and I were cousins by marriage; we had the same spiritual parents, I was his pastor, he was my children's youth pastor, we were great friends for many years, I became his boss, we had done life together for many, many years. Our relationship was healthy and full of love for each other and mutual respect.

However, one unresolved conflict led to more, birthed out of un-forgiveness and the lack of repentance. So the relationship, in my view, was very strained. It got to a point where he would stay in his office, and I would retreat to mine.

I thought there was no way of changing his mind about me, but I knew if we were to part ways, it could likely destroy the ministry into which we had both given our lives. So, we stayed together, but festering un-forgiveness from two different offices.

I deceived myself into thinking no one in the ministry could tell that I was dealing with the emotions of hurt, rejection, anger, and whatever else I was allowing to control me. But the people knew. The sad part about the people sensing the division between the two offices was that they then had to choose which office they were going to support. Neither THE MAN IN THE OFFICE NEXT DOOR nor I asked people to choose sides, intentionally, but it was still happening.

Un-forgiveness births division. This is why Jesus teaches us the Spiritual principle of forgiveness. Jesus said, *"For if you forgive other people when they sin against you, your Heavenly Father will also forgive you. But if you do not forgive others their sins, your Father will not forgive your sins."* (Matthew 6:14-15)

Forgiveness attracts forgiveness and unity. Un-forgiveness produces more un-forgiveness and division. I had forgotten that I could not be united with God and, at the same time, not forgive. I forgot that I could not experience God's forgiveness if I did not forgive others. I knew this! I preached this! However, I had embraced the *effects* of the un-forgiveness instead of realizing I was harboring un-forgiveness.

I retreated from the conflict, forgetting that retreat would never heal the wounds nor bring victory. Time does not heal all wounds, as they say. It can create numbness to pain and may even enable you to ignore the effects of the situation. But time does not heal! Only the Spirit of God can heal, and He gives us the recipe for the healing. FORGIVE and REPENT!

Every time I shut my office door, I was retreating to what I thought was a safe place. A bunker made to protect me during the war. However, what my office had become was a resting place for the enemy. It was not a place of rest for me, but a place where I validated my own pain and fear. Every time I walked straight to my office and shut the door, I acted out what was going on in the spirit realm and within the lives of the people God sent me to lead.

I showed the world that I was not mature or healthy enough to address the issues at hand and bring resolve to the situation. My focus was on me and not on the lives I was there to impact for God.

The Lord had given me the incredible opportunity to lead a vast group of people to Him, but I chose to shut a door and hide like the broken, whipped, frail man that I was. Not only that, but I lost sight of the fact that THE MAN IN THE OFFICE NEXT DOOR and his family were entrusted to me by the Lord and by our spiritual mother and father. I was not doing what I committed to do. I pushed this family away without realizing it.

My office was where I went to suppress love and guidance and express frustration and separation. THE MAN IN THE OFFICE NEXT DOOR had a beautiful wife and two children. They were a shining example of family. A godly family who loved each other, supported each other, and who did an incredible job of doing life together.

Maybe this also played into my pain and unconscious rationale for shutting myself off from them. I was confronted with the fact that I hadn't been the best husband and father.

Maybe as I watched THE MAN IN THE OFFICE NEXT DOOR being a great husband, I was envious of what he had. Possibly, I was jealous of how well he fathered his children.

At the time of the conflict, my marriage was not the best it had ever been or is now. I failed as a husband many times. Though I had never committed a great immoral sin against my wife, I did choose other things over my wife's needs at times. Ministry came first at times. Recreation came before the needs of my wife at times. I chose silly things to release the pain and stress of my downward life cycle instead of choosing my wife.

Maybe, too, I was not the dad that I could have been to my son and daughter at that time. I hadn't had my father in my home to teach me what it meant to be a good father. So maybe as I watched THE MAN IN THE OFFICE NEXT DOOR live out the life of a great dad to his children, it began to convict me to deal with my choices and failures as a dad.

Whatever I was dealing with kept me behind closed doors and murdered the relationships that I committed to lead and protect.

I had become a failure hiding in a closet.

OFFICE DOOR 2:

I've heard my whole life, "time heals all wounds." I never doubted that the wounds *could* heal. I just questioned whether they *would*. Time had passed. The pain didn't.

Day after day, it seemed like that initial crack in the

pillars from that Sunday afternoon football game continued to fracture more and more.

Although THE MAN IN THE OFFICE NEXT DOOR and I worked together, it seemed we rarely "worked together" at all. The wound seemed infected. Time wasn't healing this one.

I recall that as I came into the church office every Monday morning, I would proceed to my office and shut the door behind me. He did the same. It was like we both returned to our corners after the bell rang at the end of each round.

I felt like we were more 'business associates" than we were pastors and leaders – much less, brothers! I remember having to tell myself daily, "Marty, just clock in today, and at 5:00 pm, you get to clock out again." "Just do your job!" "Focus on the task at hand." "Get in and get out."

But on the drive home from the church office, or better yet, from my cave of calamity, I began to think to myself, "This is absurd. THE MAN IN THE OFFICE NEXT DOOR is family. How is this happening right now? To ministry leaders? To pastors? To friends? To family?"

I could never have dreamed in a million years that the wounds from the battlefield on that Sunday afternoon would ever be able to heal.

I remember the pain of having to watch our church members walk into the building and immediately dodge either me or THE MAN IN THE OFFICE NEXT DOOR. It all hinged on whether they donned the blue or the gray. There were times when people closer to him would come in, see me, drop their heads, and go straight to his office without speaking a word to me or acknowledging I was even in the room. My heart sank deeper and deeper each time.

Bitterness set in. Then rejection. Then the sting of pain would surface. Tears would flow. Then anger quickly ensued. The cycle would happen each time someone walked into our church building. My mind would say they are either for you or against you. If they were for me, I celebrated them. If they were against me, I found myself becoming very critical of them.

Still others would come in and see THE MAN IN THE OFFICE NEXT DOOR, drop their heads and proceed to my office without acknowledging him. And if I'm honest, that felt good to me. Honestly, it was like a shot of morphine that made my pain disappear. That morphine didn't last nearly as long as I had hoped because, inevitably, another would walk in, see me, drop his head, and walk on to the next office. Wash. Rinse. Repeat. Day in and day out, this continued for several years.

I'm eternally grateful for the Ministry Training Center that prepared me for the ministry. There I learned my relationship with Jesus was about a blood covenant rather than a mere contract. I gained understanding of how to study the Bible using some excellent tools like the Strong's Concordance.

Unfortunately, one of the things the Ministry Training Center didn't teach me was how to process the pain I would endure from the people I was to lead, or, in my case, lead WITH. So, I began to find myself resorting to my default settings of "retreat and delete."

I found myself running to my cave of calamity and mentally "deleting" anyone that wasn't for me. How tragic! How hypocritical! You don't have to tell me how hypocritical that was of me. Trust me. I carried that judgment daily. Hypocrisy became my scarlet letter. But through it all, I still led well. I felt that I led exceptionally well. I just bled better. I was leading while bleeding, and I knew it.

Thank God for His grace and His mercy!

It's not as though I didn't want to forgive. Trust me, I did. I wanted to laugh with him again. I wanted to hang out more outside of the church than we did inside the church. I wanted to have dinner with him and his family, my family.

Being offended, however, felt better than forgiveness. Playing the victim seemed soothing to me. I fed off of others who sympathized with me. It's tough to admit and to even think about, for that matter. That offense made me question my own salvation at times. (Spare me the emails; I'm 100 percent sure I am born again, and I have a dynamic, fantastic relationship with Jesus Christ.) But I found myself regularly playing mind games from time to time. I heard things like:

How can you be saved and have these evil thoughts toward one of your brothers in Christ?

How do you preach forgiveness to others but can't forgive others – OR ask for forgiveness from others?

How do you continue to give altar calls and allow congregants to receive prayer, repent of their sins or receive a fresh touch from the Lord, yet you are too prideful to respond to your own altar calls?

Aren't you in covenant with your brother? Sure looks

more like "co-working" to me. Marty, you look more like a hireling than you do a selfless servant in the house of God.

I would hear the voice ask, Doesn't scripture mention something about *"If you do not **forgive** men their trespasses, neither will your Father **forgive** your trespasses"* (Matthew 6:15)? Wow! Guess who's walking around unforgiven?

But even after all of these accusing voices in my head, I would still justify my un-forgiveness, solidified by the pain I was experiencing. I mean, I was right! He was wrong! Yet, I would ask myself, If that's true, why do I always feel the way I do? Why do I feel guilty from time to time? Why do I feel deep regret? He wronged me, though! And I'm totally fine with crawling in my cave daily!

Or so I tried convincing myself. Still, I noticed I began to focus on me and my pain and my shame and my this and my that.

The Lord began to speak, as well. He would say things to me like, "Just because you think you ARE right doesn't make IT right. Does it Marty?"

Oh wow! Not fair, God. That one cut. And it cut deep.

Then He would say something like, "Your actions reflect your attitude" or "Your attitude determines your altitude."

OUCH!

But then He would come back with, "But I've got so much more for you. So what that you got hurt! I did too. So what that you don't agree with everything that happened! Big deal! At the end of the day, Marty, you said you loved Me and would do anything for Me. Is forgiving THE MAN IN THE OFFICE NEXT DOOR an exclusion?"

The Lord would whisper to me, "You do know that I'm the only one who can repair this now, right? But I can't do it, Marty, if you don't allow Me to step into this situation."

Maybe a part of me wanted to remain mad. Possibly my anger was fueled by the fact that I was a bit jealous of THE MAN IN THE OFFICE NEXT DOOR. I mean, he was a much better leader in the church than I ever dreamed of being. He had way more experience in ministry than I did. Maybe I was jealous of the way he was able to preach with such power. Could jealousy be the fuel on the fire of anger that was burning within my heart? Could envy toward him be engulfing my life with bitterness?

Either way, I was still resorting to my cave – day in, day out.

LESSON LEARNED: One of the greatest misconceptions we have as human beings is to think that we are strong enough to carry offense and unhindered potential at the same time. It is impossible to carry a cross and hang from a cross at the same time. Every day, you will have to decide which you are willing to do. Every relationship every day will require someone to mount the cross and sacrifice their own will. The moment you come off the cross you will begin to carry the weight of said cross. That is a weight even Jesus could not carry alone. Offenses that go unaddressed, un-forgiveness, lack of repentance will all become carried crosses and keep you from living crucified lives.

The Café Meeting

Challenge Given - Challenge Accepted

OFFICE DOOR 2:

After eighteen years of full-time youth ministry, I can honestly say, through ninety-five percent of what we did in youth ministry – illustrated messages, retreats, conferences, every event we ever did – I've NEVER had a ministry budget, per se. NEVER!

Whenever our youth leadership team and I would dream about an illustrated message for the students or the next retreat, we would have to raise the funds to make it happen. That's just the way it was.

The Children's Ministry team always seemed to have a monthly amount they were able to spend. The Media Team had monthly expenses budgeted. The Worship Team always seemed to be able to purchase what they required for their ministry. The Café Team had a monthly budget for equipment and cups and coffee beans and syrups.

Not so with youth ministry. The youth ministry was required to raise our own funds versus having any monthly budgeting expenses. (Or so it seemed in my mind, anyway.)

I recall a time when I went to THE MAN IN THE

OFFICE NEXT DOOR with some specific needs for our youth ministry. It was during a time when I noticed our church spending "above and beyond budgeted" funds on other ministries and various general upgrades around our facility, and I thought now would be a great time to throw our ministry needs in the hat, as well. I remember stepping into his office. I felt about as nervous as a young teenage boy about to ask his Dad for his first car. (LOL)

I began to discuss these ministry needs with THE MAN IN THE OFFICE NEXT DOOR. I explained how these expenditures would only enhance our youth area and bring more excitement and "buy-in" from our leaders and students.

We had never met to discuss the financial needs of the ministry I was overseeing before now. I just knew I would get the approval and move forward with our plans to enhance our youth area and our ministry in general. I was confident. I was excited. And somewhere deep within, I felt this conversation would show him my commitment to the youth ministry, the church, and to him as my pastor and leader, that I was dreaming, teeming with vision and working hard to see growth and improvements in my department. Maybe, just maybe, this would be the very thing that allows him to see our heart for the house we were blessed to serve in.

As I began to pour out my heart, I recall feeling pretty confident. I thought to myself, Hey, we may actually be able to do this. Then I noticed he was looking down at his laptop more than at me. My confidence left as quickly as it came.

I remember him saying something to the effect of, "I

can't give you an answer today; give me some time to think about it."

I immediately thought to myself; I'm not even sure he heard much of what I said. As I walked out of his office, I had a second thought: This man hates me!

Days later, THE MAN IN THE OFFICE NEXT DOOR returned to my office with his response to my budget proposal. He came into my office and sat directly across from me on my black couch. It's funny; even as I'm writing this, it's like my mind immediately goes right back to that moment, and I can see it so vividly.

He began to share with me an idea he had come up with that may help the entire church out and not just the youth ministry. He stated that he had spoken with our Foreign Missions Team leaders and had worked something out with them. They ran our church café and used its profits to help fund missions trips and various works they were involved in.

This team was so passionate about foreign missions, and each person had invested so much time on the mission field. This café provided a beautiful, steady stream of income for them. His solution was to take the café ministry from under their direction and hand it over to me and our youth ministry so we would receive those profits from now on.

His face lit up with a smile. His heart seemed full and relieved. Mine sank.

The entire time he was unpacking his idea, my mind was saying things like, "How in the world could I live with myself and look at the Foreign Missions Team leaders and their team after this transition. I felt like they would assume that I just went crying to the senior pastor regarding funds and that I was solely responsible for not only cutting off their supply of income for ministry but now our youth ministry would benefit from all their hard work, blood, sweat and tears building the café ministry

The venom from the bite of bitterness began to sting my heart. Anger started to simmer within me. My mind went from thinking about the Foreign Missions Team to thoughts like:

- He just wants you to have to work for it

- He wants to put more on you and your team; that's all

Anger began to rise. Now, I was offended. I felt it. I got defensive.

I replied, "I can't do that."

His countenance changed almost immediately. His smile vanished. Disbelief exuded from his face. Shock had set in.

I said, "That's not an option. There is no way I can do that."

His shock soon turned to anger.

I reiterated, "I can't do that."

That anger in my heart and the utter shock in his heart (and I'm sure a feeling of dishonor) combusted into an all-out argument in no time.

Our voices got louder and louder. I thought to myself; this is it. It ends here today. All the distance between us, the lack of conversations between us, all the lunches I wasn't invited to when other staff members were – the pain was just too much! I felt like, "Speak now or forever hold your peace."

So I chose "speak now."

I began to tell him what I felt about his idea and what I thought about him. He fired right back with his feelings about me. He jumped up and began to walk out of my office, and I followed his every step. I just came to the conclusion: If this is it, I'm going out with a bang. I won't pull any punches at all. If we argue, we argue. If we fight, we fight.

Voices got louder. Words grew viler by the second. Within minutes, our rage left us both willing to forsake all and go in for the kill.

We both hurled brutal words at each other. Although the punches were verbal, the impact felt extremely physical. Back and forth we went in a ring of rage. We had finally come to the point of squaring off toe-to-toe, and both threw some pretty nasty haymakers from the opening bell.

Round after round we went. He would throw an uppercut from being thoroughly upset. I would counter with a straight right jab of bitter resentment. Eyes began to swell shut. Lips busted. Noses bloody. Don't think words don't hurt.

To be honest, however, it felt good. For once in my life, I spoke up for what I felt was right. I had been pushed around and bullied for most of my life. NOT TODAY! We went after it.

Again, our punches were verbal, not physical. They were emotionally charged, vindictive, and marinated in malice. Each word was a connecting punch that landed with great force and stung like alcohol hitting an open wound. But we kept swinging for the fence with each opportunity.

The fight lasted less than a couple of minutes. Maybe half a round or so. It felt like an eternity in the ring. Outside we were fine, but it was as if we were both a bloody mess on the inside.

The last punch was thrown by THE MAN IN THE OFFICE NEXT DOOR. It would prove to be a knockout blow. The judge stopped the fight. The bell rang. It was all over. Two devastating shots knocked me out: "YOU'RE FIRED!"

I picked myself up off the mat and walked back to my corner (aka my office). I was wounded. I couldn't breathe. Bloody. Despised. Dejected. Done.

After a few minutes of catching my breath and calming down in my corner, I thought to myself, Did that really just happen? I think I would rather have been in a physical confrontation. This verbal onslaught was one billion times more painful. I felt betrayed. I felt unwanted. I felt abandoned. I felt alone. I grabbed my keys and headed for the door.

Once I was in the car, I called my wife and said, "Well, it's over. I'm done here."

That was the moment reality set in. I remember thinking, Was that my last time stepping foot in this church? Would I ever be back? What about our teenagers in the youth ministry? What about ministry? Is this it for me? What will happen now? How do we salvage this ministry, or better yet, this relationship? Is this beyond repair? Do I even want to fix it?

Wow, my once fiery, burning heart was now growing cold.

Days would go by with deadly silence. Not a word would be spoken between us. In my mind, it was time to roll the credits. It was over.

OFFICE DOOR 1:

THE MAN IN THE OFFICE NEXT DOOR *came to me with a budgeting issue he was having, trying to fund his* vision for our youth ministry.

My heart was still for him. I loved him and wanted him to succeed. Despite all the confusion and emotion, I believed in THE MAN IN THE OFFICE NEXT DOOR. I knew there was greatness in him. I had seen it manifest many times over.

I am a person who thrives on helping others fulfill their dreams, so when he approached me with the need for funds, I immediately began to strategize. I wanted to be the hero for THE MAN IN THE OFFICE NEXT DOOR, his family, and his ministry. I began to rack my brain on what I could make happen for him. I came up with what I thought was an incredible opportunity.

Our ministry had a café that served coffee and light snacks, breakfast items, and little specialty drinks before Sunday services. At the time, it was being run by our foreign missions ministry. So I met with the foreign missions ministers and told them I would allow the youth ministry to take over the café, and all the proceeds would go straight to the youth ministry to use as they saw fit.

The foreign ministry pastors embraced the concept and supported it without hesitation. I could not have been more excited. Maybe this would be the very thing that would allow THE MAN IN THE OFFICE NEXT DOOR to see my heart for him and begin the healing process between us!

With excitement and great anticipation, I walked from my office to his. I knocked on the closed door and heard him say, "Come in."

I remember sitting down in a black office chair in front of his desk. I remember feeling like a mixture of "This is it!" and being called to the principal's office as a child.

I began to explain how I would give the café ministry to the youth ministry to run for the profits. I said that I had it all worked out, meaning that I met with the ministers who had operated the café and were on board.

I gave him the strategy, and then I sat back in that old black chair, proud of myself and awaiting his praise and gratitude. As I looked at him, probably with a grin of pride, he began to shake his head from side to side. Then his first words – the words I had been waiting to hear for several days were, "No, I am not going to do that."

My grin immediately turned into a red face, a psychopathic face. He began to tell me that it was not a blessing for him and the youth ministry to run the café, but more work than value. He said they were not going to be on board with the idea.

I remember thinking of all the sermons I had heard and preached on submission to authority. In a moment, I felt a thousand emotions come over me. All the feelings from the last few years of built-up anger came to a crescendo. I wish I could articulate the moment and restate my response, but honestly, I don't remember. However, I do remember thinking to myself that if I don't get out of this office, I will hurt someone and/or myself!

See, I am from Duluth, Georgia. For you who may not know, Duluth, Georgia, is in the heart of Southern USA. The deep south. My point is, I grew up thinking every conflict was settled with a fight. When a dispute arose, it was time to "scratch some gravel." Or, in other words, fight!

I did not want to fight my brother. The last thing I wanted to do was strike him, but I felt the challenge was given, so the challenge was accepted. Now we did not physically fight – thank the Lord! The meeting ended with us screaming at each other as we exited the office area and into the foyer.

Standing in the foyer was a member of our ministry. She stood all about four feet, nine inches tall, and her eyes were as big as basketballs.

We didn't care!

He told me what he thought about me and the situation, and I let him know the same.

My heart breaks as I even think about this confrontation. The hurt we both were experiencing. The rejection we both felt. Two brothers ejected into a situation for which neither of us was prepared. Years of love and respect for each other were gone in a moment.

I told THE MAN IN THE OFFICE NEXT DOOR that he was fired and to get out of the church building. I was big and bad! I was THE MAN, and no one was going to speak to me like he was and get away with it.

I acted like I was in full control and full authority. I had my chest stuck out and had the attitude it was my way or the highway. Or at least that's what I portrayed.

I left the foyer area and returned to my office. I then called our pastor and spiritual father on the phone to let him know what had happened. The moment I heard the voice of our pastor on the phone, my hard shell crumbled. The man who stood in the foyer of a church and fired his brother with passion and certainty was now crying like a baby. I told our pastor, "I just fired your boy!"

At this point, I was shaking uncontrollably, crying profusely, and wishing I could get back the last ten minutes of my life to do it all over again. But the damage was done.

Pastor asked me what had happened, and I told him my story. It was as accurate as I could tell it. I didn't try to make THE MAN IN THE OFFICE NEXT DOOR out to be the bad guy. Our pastor knew of the conflict between me and THE MAN IN THE OFFICE NEXT DOOR. He knew us both very, very well. I didn't want to pass the blame. I wanted people to know I was not innocent in the situation, but I also wanted people to know I was hurt while trying to make things work.

I hadn't wanted us to walk away from the meeting divided. My heart had been to bring an answer to the table that would help THE MAN IN THE OFFICE NEXT DOOR. I had envisioned the meeting going a lot differently than it did, but now we had both reacted like two little boys on an elementary school playground, fighting over who was going to slide down the slide first.

I had felt challenged, as though everything I was trained to believe about honor, respect, and spiritual authority was challenged, and that I had to respond. I didn't want to be like Ahab, the king married to a woman named Jezebel. She may have been the most hate-filled lady ever to live. She killed people and even killed the prophets of God. One of the saddest things about Jezebel's story is that her husband Ahab, the king, would never stand up to her.

I was taught that leaders who do not stand up to rebellion or disagreement were like Ahab. I didn't want to be a bad leader. I didn't want to allow rebellion to be mingled with God's anointing in our house and ruin the people. So, when I felt THE MAN IN THE OFFICE NEXT DOOR acted rebelliously, I hit it head-on.

However, I handled the situation wrongfully. I escalated the situation to its highest pitch, and, instead of trying to see things from his point of view, I reacted out of my own need for control, and I hurt the very person and people I was trying to protect. I had failed the test!

Now THE MAN IN THE OFFICE NEXT DOOR was not around for me to apologize to. I couldn't make things right because I had drawn a line that would, unfortunately, take years to erase.

LESSON LEARNED: Monumental moments in life are most often erected from more simple situations. There is nothing that can build quicker and with more force than unresolved anger. Hidden anger will come out! It oftentimes manifests at the most crucial times of our lives. We get angry at work and instead of addressing it then, we bring it home to our spouse or children. The dinner table then becomes a metaphoric board room and the wrong people are "fired" from our lives. Anger wrongly directed will surely hit the mark. Unresolved anger or pain is not shot from the barrel of a single-shot gun but most always sprays violently as though coming from an automatic weapon! Deal with your offenses, anger, un-forgiveness, and conflict before your tiptoeing through the tulips becomes you wading through the blood-soaked chasms of a war zone.

Meeting with the Head Honcho

The Pain of Separation

OFFICE DOOR 1:

I received a call from our pastor a few days after the café meeting. He asked for me and THE MAN IN THE OFFICE NEXT DOOR to come and meet with him and try to resolve the issues between us. The turmoil between THE MAN IN THE OFFICE NEXT DOOR and me was now drawing in other people by the minute.

I had fooled myself into thinking the conflict between us was simply between us and, one day, would work itself out. I failed to realize that any conflict left unaddressed will grow out of control on its own.

Conflict breeds on its own strength. Our failure to address it, deal with it, and bring a resolution to it gives life to conflict. I convinced myself that the love THE MAN IN THE OFFICE NEXT DOOR and I had for each other at one time would be strong enough to eventually breakthrough.

Man, was I wrong!

When I arrived at our pastor's office, I immediately saw the pain on his face. I could tell the conflict between his sons weighed on him. I was already very uneasy for many reasons, being filled with emotions.

The last time I had seen THE MAN IN THE OFFICE NEXT DOOR was when he walked out of our church building as we yelled at each other. I was trying to sift through all kinds of emotions – anger, hurt, fear, rejection, and so on. It also didn't help that my pastor's office was filled wall to wall with University of Alabama photos and souvenirs. As a huge University of Georgia fan, the environment put me on edge even more. I can sense the emotions coming back right now, even as I recall that day! (Joking, of course, kinda.)

We all three sat down, and our pastor asked us what was going on. Both of us were hesitant to be the first to open a conversation that was sure to uncover months and months of buried frustration, so we both eased our way into releasing our sides of the events leading up to the meeting.

Honestly, I would love to tell you everything that was said in that meeting. I would love to articulate how I defended my actions, expressed my concerns, and proved that I was right about the whole ordeal. However, I can't remember what was said. I don't remember any of the logistics of the conversation that lasted well over an hour, maybe two. All I remember is the pain, the brokenness, and the crumbs of potential that now littered the carpet of a private, not well-decorated office.

I do remember that at one point, the meeting climaxed with our pastor and THE MAN IN THE OFFICE NEXT DOOR in a disagreement. All of a sudden, the dam burst open. THE MAN IN THE OFFICE NEXT DOOR stood up and began to walk out of the office. He said he was quitting the ministry and everything. He wasn't rebellious or insubordinate. He was hurting and confused, and I am sure he felt cornered.

At that moment, I saw the pain of separation. The head honcho – our pastor – broke down in tears and begged his son not to leave and to please come back and sit down so that we could bring closure to this meeting. At that point, I think we all became emotional.

I watched as three young, strong, wise, experienced, proven leaders – men of God – broke under the power of un-forgiveness and unresolved issues.

Pastor asked me to leave the room, and, for close to an hour, he met alone with THE MAN IN THE OFFICE NEXT DOOR. I stood in a nearby restroom and broke. I could not bear to see my pastor, my spiritual father, the only man who, for over twenty years, had been a daddy to me, weep because of the stark division between his sons.

I was later welcomed back into the room, where the atmosphere had changed somewhat. Pastor was not weeping anymore. THE MAN IN THE OFFICE NEXT DOOR had a whole other look about him. We left that meeting with an agreement to try one more time to move beyond our conflicts. THE MAN IN THE

OFFICE NEXT DOOR told me he had never given me his heart and that he had not entirely given his heart to our ministry, but he would try.

I told him I was sorry for my mistakes, and we left.

I don't know about THE MAN IN THE OFFICE NEXT DOOR, but I was not honest. I did not truly repent. I wanted things to be different. I did not want my brother hurt and isolated any longer, but I felt I was done, that he had done too much damage.

I left the meeting knowing I would be right back in this place within a few weeks. In essence, I lied to us all. I wanted so badly to believe my brother and I were okay and that we would do ministry together for a long time. However, I "protected" myself by holding on to the walls I had built in case it didn't work out.

I did something I preached for years not to do. I planned for failure. I gave myself a way of escape. I prepared for an ending that eventually happened, not necessarily because of anything that would have happened on its own, but because I could not honestly release myself and my brother from what had already happened.

As was inevitable under the circumstances, the cycle repeated itself. However, this next time, the cycle had picked up steam and was not a storm, but a hurricane!

OFFICE DOOR 2:

I received a phone call from our senior pastor stating he wanted to meet with me and THE MAN IN THE OFFICE NEXT DOOR. He knew this could not go any further without a calm conversation with hopes of restoring our relationship. He knew there were far more parties involved and affected than just the two of us who fought like children on a playground just days before. It was like a father calling his two boys into the living room after they began scuffling over a toy in a back bedroom.

As the meeting began, our senior pastor did his very best to diffuse the situation. He truly did. As the three of us sat in his office, you could cut the tension between the two of us with a knife. Emotions were still present in both parties. Highly present. Anger was leading the charge, with rejection close behind. Hurt and bitterness lurked in the shadows, and unforgiveness was bringing up the rear. The emotions were all there, though they were caged up at the moment.

I think our senior pastor was hoping for a miracle to happen and that we would be able to make it past this horrific encounter. I mean, our senior pastor was accustomed to seeing people in this exact situation confessing one to another, repenting, hugging it out, and then going for coffee. That would not be the case in this particular meeting.

As the meeting progressed (regressed?), THE MAN IN THE OFFICE NEXT DOOR and I began to share our versions of what had transpired over the last several days, months, and even years. When I spoke, I spoke with great passion regarding how hurt I was, how left out I felt, how right I was, and how wrong THE MAN IN THE OFFICE NEXT DOOR was.

When THE MAN IN THE OFFICE NEXT DOOR spoke, I tuned him out until he began to sound like Charlie Brown's school teacher to me, as I chose to hear nothing but jumbled jargon.

I recall a moment in the meeting that I felt like our senior pastor took sides with THE MAN IN THE OFFICE NEXT DOOR. I don't remember exactly how it was said, but I remember hearing something like this, "I can't have this. Marty. If you don't fix this, you'll need to find something else. I just can't have this."

Again, I'm positive this is not exactly how he said it, but once you've allowed yourself to be baptized in bitterness, your ears tend to hear things differently.

Wow! *I* have to fix this? *I* do? Or find something *else*? Okay, I thought to myself, instead of one opponent in the ring, now I have two. In a split second, I found myself on my feet and making my way to the door for my exit. I blew up like a hand grenade.

Was I confused? Absolutely! I knew I didn't get us into this mess alone. Why was it all of a sudden my responsibility to "fix it"?

Mad? As a hornet!

Rebellious? You better believe it! I wanted to get my hands on a door or two, or ten. I would slam every single one of them until they rattled the rafters.

Why? Because that's what would feel good. Let me break a door off of its hinges. That would feel wonderful. Our senior pastor, the "Head Honcho," called for me before I could get my hand on the door handle. He asked me not to leave like that. He pleaded with me; as tears came to his eyes and his voice cracked, he asked me to stay and try to work this out together. We all began to weep. Emotions were high. Extremely high. Code Red-type high.

I reminded myself of a life lesson my mentor for the past decade or so taught me. Jeanne Mayo would say, "Marty, HURTING people HURT people! Never forget that."

None of the three sitting there in that office that day had been prepared for a meeting like this. Neither Bible college, seminary, nor any ministry training center can equip you for battlefields quite like this one. It is precisely in moments like these, as humans, we tend to revert to old ways of doing things, and human tendencies seem always to kick in and override any other coping mechanisms. We get defensive. Resentment sets in. Our reaction to adversity is through the lens and mindset of "fight or flight." Run away or swing. Leave the room or lash out against everyone in your way.

Offense has no prejudice. It doesn't consult with you to see if you have a college degree or not. Offense doesn't call ahead of time to reserve a table with you and doesn't ask if you've memorized scripture or if you've had a quiet time lately. Offense has this dark, evil, vindictive way of convincing you that when someone hurts you deeply, your reaction should always be to build a wall between you and the one who offended you to protect you from ever having to experience that kind of pain again. Offense will cause you to build a fence!

After some discussion alone with my senior pastor, I agreed to try to work things out with THE MAN IN THE OFFICE NEXT DOOR. Once the three of us came back together, we all agreed to do our parts to make this relationship work – for our families, for our churches, for ourselves.

We verbally communicated our commitment to try to make things work. But I think, deep down, we all knew, no matter how hard we scooped buckets of water and threw it overboard, this vessel was destined for disaster.

Our working relationship had just taken on too much water. Little did either of us know just how quick this ship would sink.

LESSON LEARNED: Un-forgiveness and unresolved anger WILL KILL YOU! We are not designed to carry these types of issues, nor to be people who carry un-forgiveness and harbor hate and anger.

The Bible says in 2 Corinthians 5:14-21, *"Either way, Christ's love controls us. Since we believe that Christ died for all, we also believe that we have all died to our old life. He died for everyone so that those who receive his new life will no longer live for themselves. Instead, they will live for Christ, who died and was raised for them. So we have stopped evaluating others from a human point of view. At one time we thought of Christ merely from a human point of view. How differently we know him now! This means that anyone who belongs to Christ has become a new person. The old life is gone; a new life has begun! And all of this is a gift from God, who brought us back to himself through Christ. And God has given us this task of reconciling people to him. For God was in Christ, reconciling the world to himself, no longer counting people's sins against them. And he gave us this wonderful message of reconciliation. So we are Christ's ambassadors; God is making his appeal through us. We speak for Christ when we plead, 'Come back to God!' For God made Christ, who never sinned, to be the offering for our sin, so that we could be made right with God through Christ."* (NLT)

I Don't Need Him Anyway

Am I My Brother's Keeper?

> Offense is an event. Offended is a choice.
> *Steven Furtick*

OFFICE DOOR 2:

I returned to the church offices the following week. My expectations were high. Wait a minute. Who am I kidding? Although we were back in the church office "together," there was an obvious chasm between us. It was a deep chasm. A dark chasm.

Offense is not, in itself, deadly until we allow it to mature. When it morphs from an offense that happened TO us to acceptance of deep offense within us, that offense now has the power and potential to produce the poisonous fruit of anger, resentment, bitterness, strife, envy, and jealousy. These are just a few of the toxic outgrowths offense introduces into your life.

I knew this. I just never expected to have to navigate these waters for myself.

It's not as though I desired to have these feelings at all. I never asked for this fruit. I wasn't afforded the luxury of choosing the fruit; I merely chose what to do with the seed sown. Once the seed of offense was sown, it began to germinate in the soil of self-preservation, and I immediately found myself going into "protect and defend" mode.

Nothing THE MAN IN THE OFFICE NEXT DOOR did was right from that moment forward. It didn't matter what it was; I "wronged" every single one of his "rights." Let me explain.

If THE MAN IN THE OFFICE NEXT DOOR preached a breath-taking message on a Sunday morning and the congregation was standing and applauding wildly, I found myself seated, reserved, and quiet. If THE MAN IN THE OFFICE NEXT DOOR spoke up during a staff meeting and cracked a joke so that the entire staff and support staff laughed along with him, I sat puckered and pouting. I know, it seems so childish, so second grade, but it was my reality. It wasn't that I didn't truly love THE MAN IN THE OFFICE NEXT DOOR; honestly, I did love him through all of this. I just didn't like him anymore.

WOW! Just having to see myself type this out on my laptop brought tears to my eyes. How hateful! How self-absorbed! How petty! How broken!

I had always taken pride in serving well. However, after this offense took root in my soul, I found myself not offering my help to him anymore. I stopped going the extra mile for him. I found myself thinking, "He's a grown man; if he needs something, he can get it himself. And if he needs something done, he can do it himself."

It grieves me to admit this, but that's where I was. When you feel as if you've been betrayed, your actions can become brutal.

How could two men who loved God and each other allow so much division to come between them? So much so that the thriving ministry they once led together had become burdensome. Our individual ministries were doing well. Ministry together, not so much. The tension between us was as hard as steel. And looking back, our once-solid relationship seemed to have turned to quicksand overnight. The more we fought and tried to salvage our relationship, the more we sank deeper and deeper.

I found myself not only distancing myself from him more and more, but I was quickly developing this "forget him" mentality, and I became quick-tempered toward THE MAN IN THE OFFICE NEXT DOOR.

My attitude had become "Cain-like" in nature. (Cain was the brother of Abel in the book of Genesis.) Cain was a worker of the ground. Abel was a keeper of sheep. Abel, a shepherd; Cain, a farmer. Abel fed and groomed. Cain plowed and harvested. Both were gifted in their own right. Both served their house well. Both loved their parents. Both did their part to provide. I'm sure they both worked hard. No doubt, both loved the Lord. I mean, they both brought Him an offering. Cain cultivated the ground, planted the seed, and gathered the harvest. He offered God the fruits of his labor. He just knew God would be impressed by his offering. Abel, on the other hand, said, "God, I didn't do a thing. You created this precious lamb, and I'm just offering back to You what is already Yours."

It was as if Cain expected a blessing from God, as though God owed him something in return. Abel, on the other hand, was offering to the Lord what the Lord had created and was giving back to the Lord what belonged to Him, assuming credit for nothing.

When the Lord accepted Abel's posture of giving and not Cain's, Cain became enraged and turned against his brother. So Cain attacked and killed Abel. Afterward, the Lord asked Cain where his brother was (because the Lord said he heard Abel's blood crying out to Him from the ground) and Cain responded, "I don't know. Am I my brother's keeper?" A curse came upon Cain at that very moment.

When we deliberately choose not to extend grace to others, withhold forgiveness instead of releasing it to others, and allow bitterness and resentment to enter our lives due to others' actions, we open the doorway for a curse to come upon us, as Cain did.

I felt like this particular passage of scripture fit our story more than any other. Two men. No, two brothers. Two individuals. Two sons. Two different skill sets. Two different callings. Two different thought processes. "Two different" was easily translated "too different" for me and THE MAN IN THE OFFICE NEXT DOOR.

Although we had so much in common together, we consistently drifted apart with our differences. Even though we were on a church staff together and in the same family (THE MAN IN THE OFFICE NEXT DOOR married my first cousin), I found myself pushing him further away as each day passed.

I felt as if he had already formed alliances with other staff members and many church members. I recall numerous occasions during a typical work week where THE MAN IN THE OFFICE NEXT DOOR would go to lunch with other male staff members, excluding me, whereas, previously, it had been common for us to go together. Many times on Sunday mornings or Wednesday nights, I rounded a corner to find THE MAN IN THE OFFICE NEXT DOOR in conversation with a couple of our church members, who then seemed to stop talking until I walked away.

Having dealt with rejection in my past, this only seemed to add fuel to the fire. It became very apparent that two different camps were forming in our midst. Our church body seemed to be splitting into three groups: those that sided with him, those that sided with me, and those who had no idea what was going on. It's not that they chose "sides" per se; it was more like they were choosing offices. Nor was it something they did intentionally or that had been forced upon them.

I think we humans tend toward taking sides in any issue, leaning to one camp or the other organically, subliminally, relationally. Maybe it is in our DNA. It seems natural to lean one way or the other in any circumstance or situation.

Division had crept its way into our offices and had left an ugly stain on our two or the church staff members (THE MAN IN THE OFFICE NEXT DOOR and me), and now that same division had found a way to have a direct negative impact on our church. The division affected our entire church, and now it was coming for our friends - and worse yet, our families.

The Lord could not be pleased with our disunity. Relationships all around us were on the verge of massive unraveling due to our un-forgiveness. And to think, all of this grew from two grown men bickering on a ball field!

It didn't take long at all for division to appear on every platform: at church, family functions (birthday parties, holidays, etc.), and in public gatherings. It was evident, and everyone felt its sting.

The thoughts in my mind added compound interest to my frustrations and anger towards THE MAN IN THE OFFICE NEXT DOOR. I harbored thoughts such as, "If he's such a man of God, why doesn't he try to fix this?" Or, "He is the Senior Pastor of this church. He can swoop in and help others with their failing relationships, but he doesn't seem to have the words to bring restoration to ours. How is that?" "Why does he not care enough to repent to me and fight for our relationship?"

As frequently as those thoughts came to my mind, voices from another direction chimed in, too. They would say things like, "You are a pastor too! What are you doing to help rebuild this relationship?" Or more gut-wrenching, "How can you stand and preach from the sacred desk, the pulpit, and be full of resentment, bitterness, un-forgiveness, and anger?" "How can you preach unity, yet separate yourself from your senior pastor?" "Marty, don't you know and believe the book you preach from every week?" "Haven't you read Mark 3:25? You do know that a house divided against itself cannot stand, right, Marty?"

That was the battleground of my thought life. As you probably know, the thought life is just as real and active as the lives we live out daily in front of others. Our emotions affect our thoughts, and our thoughts tend to shape our lives.

When unresolved conflict enters through the doorway

of our emotions, it begins to entertain itself with the intent of building massive momentum in our minds until it takes root in our hearts.

Unresolved conflict can and should be dealt with and terminated in the "emotions" phase. Once it has gone through "the mind" phase and has picked up steam, it hits the heart, where roots are grown. If it continues unresolved, conflict will require tons of time and undivided attention that the vast majority won't or can't invest for resolution.

The constant attention and tools required to cut away the twisted branches of bitterness can seem out of reach and impossible. It's like an extreme hoarder who desperately wants to clean his house but has no idea where to begin, and neither the time nor energy for.

The roots that have woven themselves into the heart can become so dominant that they seem too much to bear. They can feel overwhelming.

Sometimes I wonder how it ever got to be so out of control. I feel so guilty even reflecting on all of this. The wreckage and aftermath we left in our wake, with everyone that knew and loved both of us, was enormous. We could not get along, and that weighed heavily on everyone around us.

Our actions had left others at an awkward place of not knowing which one of us to speak to for fear of upsetting the other. Everyone walked on eggshells around us. The soil around us was so unstable. My heart breaks for anyone who has drunk from this cup of offense. Whether you drank deliberately or accidentally, the intoxicating ingredients remain the same. They are unprejudiced; they are equal opportunity offenders.

If you have animosity towards anyone, please deal with it NOW! Don't wait another day. The longer you put it off, the longer it has permission to hang around and have lethal effects on everyone involved. If this is speaking to you right now and you can think of someone you have ought with, someone you haven't spoken to in quite a while due to unresolved conflict, please, put this book down immediately, pick up the phone, and contact them RIGHT NOW!

Repent as you look for their number. Ask for forgiveness, even as you begin to call them. Allow the Lord back into that relationship so He can start the process of restoration.

The Lord longs for the restoration of broken relationships. From cover to cover, the Bible reveals broken people and broken relationships that God desires to mend. Not only that, He asks us to partner with Him during the entire process. You can partner with Him today by making the call or sending the text. Holy Spirit may even ask you to go in person to make things right.

Although I had convinced myself that I was not my "brother's keeper," deep down in my heart, I wanted to be his keeper. I found myself being agitated with him while desiring his friendship again. I remember going to the office day in and day out with our staff, with him, with others, yet I was feeling so lonely.

Why does it have to be this way? Why is it much easier to stay offended with each other than it is to reconcile? Why does it feel so good to play the victim in this scenario? Why do I drop subtle hints to others that they need to side with me and take up my offense as well?

These were the questions I was asking myself weekly. But, the greatest of all was this question right here, "Why can't I truly forgive him?"

Sure, I *said* I forgave him "in my heart," but I knew I hadn't. That kind of talk was great church jargon. You cannot forgive someone "in your heart" and still walk around bitter at them. You cannot forgive someone "in your heart" and choose not to speak to them. I had preached forgiveness for nearly two decades. I had met with countless others over the years who had issues with others and walked them through the process of forgiving the other so they could move forward and walk in freedom once again. I just could not seem to get myself to that place I had led others to time and time again.

I knew what Jesus said regarding forgiving others. In the book of Matthew, He said to forgive seventy times seven. It's one thing to be a hearer of the Word, but being a doer is another story. Un-forgiveness was the poison I was drinking, thinking it was killing him. In reality, it was killing me.

OFFICE DOOR 1:

I am not sure if it is an internal, subliminal self-protective instinct or what, but we humans have something in our make-up that we naturally protect ourselves from loss. It's as though we sense when loss or separation is coming and, without premeditation, our emotions close down, and our minds begin to plan life on the other side of the loss.

Even though I honestly and purely loved THE MAN

IN THE OFFICE NEXT DOOR, I went into self-preservation mode and closed myself off from him. It was not like a choice I made. I mean, in the end, it was the choice we both made that got us to that point, but it was not like I reviewed answers to a multiple-choice question and chose to cut him out of my life as the best choice.

He was and still is someone whom I admire in so many ways. He is a great leader, an inspiring speaker, and exceptional at anything he sets out to do. Maybe this was also something I was trying to work through. Perhaps I had made him such an example that his successes became a negative thing to me in many areas. I am not quite sure.

I wasn't sure what was going on with us when the conflict was smoldering. I still don't have many answers today. I know this one thing: I reached a point where I made up my mind that I didn't need him in my life anyway.

I came to a place where I shut off THE MAN IN THE OFFICE NEXT DOOR. Mentally, emotionally, spiritually, and eventually relationally, I shut him off.

Again, let me make it clear: I never stopped loving and believing in him! I think I felt that he, his family, and those close to him hated me so much that I had to cut my feelings for them off to survive this transition.

I can kind of see how everything played out between Cain and Abel. The Cain and Abel story is found in the Bible, in the book of Genesis. They were brothers. They played together, worked together, and grew up together. In many ways, this was good, but in some ways, it was not. The longer we stay in relationship with people, the more we get to see their humanity and are exposed to their failures. Often, we remember people for the things they have done wrong rather than what they have done right.

It is harder to outlive a mistake than it is to relive a success. In the church world, this is a principle that holds even more truth. Someone in the church world can live years as a good, holy, righteous person, but you let that person have one moment of weakness, and we will define them by that moment forever.

Cain and Abel became so familiar with each other they began to use each other for their gain. Cain and Abel brought offerings unto the Lord. Abel's heart and offering were acceptable to God, but He did not accept Cain's motives and offering. Cain was so mad at Abel that he ended up killing his brother.

When the Spirit of the Lord came to Cain, He asked Cain where his brother Able was. The Spirit of the Lord said He heard Abel's blood crying out to Him from the ground. Cain's reply to God was, "Am I my brother's keeper?"

In effect, He was saying, "I have cut him out of my life because I don't need him anyway." God was very upset about Cain's actions and response, so a curse came upon Cain.

When we allow ourselves to cut people out of our lives, a curse comes upon us, as well. It is a curse that repels forgiveness from our lives because we have no way to repent to those we have cut off. As I stated earlier, without the giving of forgiveness, it cannot be experienced.

I got to a place that, even though THE MAN IN THE OFFICE NEXT DOOR was a parishioner of mine, a cousin, a friend, a member of my staff, and a true brother, I felt I didn't need him in my life any longer. I knew that he and those closest to him had made the same decision in their hearts, as well.

What happens when a group of people turn on each other and cut each other off is that they give way to familiar spirits. Familiar spirits are attracted to people who migrate to others with commonalities, such as having the same unresolved issues. Familiar spirits attach themselves to un-forgiveness, anger, depression, and the like and influence other people who are being ruled by those same unresolved issues.

There were two camps within our ministry. It was not something that either of us I set out to create. Nevertheless, it was happening. Division was in the house, manifesting among the staff and leaders, and filtering through the whole church body. Without speaking it out, THE MAN IN THE OFFICE NEXT DOOR and I had drawn a line in the sand, and people knew they had to pick a side.

The family was separated, friends were lost, ministry was stifled, and God was dishonored. What began at a flag football game was now dividing even the closest of family and friends. No one had to say a word, but you could sense the division in the house.

I was not wise enough or spiritual enough to destroy the wall between us and put an end to this once and for all. I was the shepherd of the house. I was the "angel" God put over the house. I was the lad who led the enemy to the pillars of the house and gave him permission to feel them. I could not see this taking place at the time; I could only sense it.

I was trained in the Word and spiritual principles

enough to know what was happening. However, I was too close to the forest to see the trees, as some say.

It breaks my heart now to know how I failed all those people. Whoever you are reading this book, I beg you, do whatever you have to do to make things right with anyone from whom you are divided! I beg you to stop reading this book and go NOW to your enemy and repent to him or her!

Jesus said when we come to the altar to offer worship unto God, and we remember our brother has something against us, leave our sacrifice and make things right with our brother. Once we make things right, then and only then can we come and worship God with our offering. (Matthew 5:24)

Why couldn't I fix it and make it work? Why was I not a better leader? My leadership abilities and my spiritual authority ceased the moment I was okay with believing I didn't need him anyway.

I look back now and I remember very vividly all the emotions I was dealing with during the months of conflict with THE MAN IN THE OFFICE NEXT DOOR. At times, I would be angry, feel rejected, or even feel validated because I was the victim, of course. At other times I would feel lonely. There were still other times that I would justify my un-forgiveness. I would tell myself, "I have forgiven him in my heart." But I never went to him and really apologized.

The Lord showed me in scripture that repentance and forgiveness are impossible without humbling oneself to the point of a face-to-face, open discussion.

Jesus said it like this in Matthew 5:21-24, *"You have*

heard that it was said to those of old, 'You shall not murder, and whoever murders will be in danger of the judgment.' But I say to you that whoever is angry with his brother without a cause shall be in danger of the judgment. And whoever says to his brother, 'Raca!' shall be in danger of the council. But whoever says, 'You fool!' shall be in danger of hell fire. <u>Therefore if you bring your gift to the altar, and there remember that your brother has something against you, leave your gift there before the altar, and go your way. First be reconciled to your brother, and then come and offer your gift</u>."

You can't stay at the altar and "forgive in your heart"! You must go and make things right face to face. Now, if you are holding un-forgiveness against someone who is deceased, then, of course, we must repent and forgive within our own heart and emotions. But you cannot cop out of a Kingdom principle because your pride says otherwise.

For years, I had convinced myself that I had forgiven THE MAN IN THE OFFICE NEXT DOOR and everyone who had chosen to take his side. For years, I was bound by un-forgiveness, and I never realized it.

LESSON LEARNED: Forgiveness is NOT a recommendation from God. It is a requirement. If refusing to forgive someone can stop the eternal flow of God's Grace into your life (Matthew 6:15), then it is absolutely more powerful than anything you can handle or navigate through. Be quick to forgive! Make forgiveness a lifestyle. Learn to forgive even before you have to make a decision to.

The Dismissal

The Last Time We Spoke

OFFICE DOOR 1:

Without a doubt, the hardest meeting I have ever had was this one. I called for a meeting with THE MAN IN THE OFFICE NEXT DOOR. I also asked my CFO at the time to meet with us. It was a meeting that I had put off for way too long. I was so torn. I knew that the relationship between me and THE MAN IN THE OFFICE NEXT DOOR could not continue to go on like it was. I could see the division amongst my staff, our leadership, and even within the church body.

As the senior pastor, I knew I had to step up and somehow bring closure to the conflict. I had so much anger, rejection, fear, and a whole pile of emotions that I was struggling with, but I loved THE MAN IN THE OFFICE NEXT DOOR. I loved his wife and his children. I didn't want to hurt them in any way. I didn't want to hurt my staff or our church family, either. But as Jesus said, *"A kingdom divided against itself shall fall, and a house divided against itself shall not stand."* (Matthew 12:25)

I carried the weight of hundreds of lives upon my shoulders. I fasted, I prayed, I cried, and I sought counsel concerning the conflict between us. I knew there was only one thing I could do. There had to be a clean break between us, at least for a while. I never dreamed it would have lasted so long. I could never have imagined the emotional pain that everyone involved would have to face. I didn't want THE MAN IN THE OFFICE NEXT DOOR out of my life, but I knew things had gotten too bad to mend without change.

THE MAN IN THE OFFICE NEXT DOOR, my CFO, and I met in my office. I was confident in my decision, and I knew the meeting had the potential of becoming very volatile, especially after the café incident. So I went into the meeting very nervous but focused and determined not to lose my cool.

As I informed THE MAN IN THE OFFICE NEXT DOOR of my decision to dismiss him of his duties at the church, I waited with nervous anticipation for his response. I could only imagine what he was feeling. I am not sure if he saw the dismissal coming or not. Part of me thought he doubted I had the boldness or the heart to dismiss him. Honestly, I almost didn't. It was one of the hardest things I ever did in my life. One thought drove me: that the people who trusted us with their lives were in the balance. I was sure that I was making the correct decision, but I was also certain that I was at fault for allowing everything to escalate to this point.

I was fighting back the desire to fall down and cry out, "Why can't we just make everything better?" But I knew it would do no good. So I waited for THE MAN IN THE OFFICE NEXT DOOR to respond after informing him of my decision. He didn't respond to me directly. Instead, he took his surprise, anger, and months of frustration out on our CFO. I think he had so much he wanted to say, and he didn't want to come at me or dishonor me, so he released all his emotion onto the only other person in the room.

Once more, I found myself in a meeting where the people stuck in the middle of us were the ones experiencing heartache. I watched as my CFO wept because of the conflict between us. He had been sucked headlong into the sewage of our childishness, and now the unresolved issues were destroying another relationship on its way out.

You see, my CFO had been mentored in part by THE MAN IN THE OFFICE NEXT DOOR. He was a very seasoned businessman. He had been in controversial meetings many times in the secular world. But he had never been exposed to this type of conflict regarding the church. To say it took him by surprise is an understatement. He couldn't understand why he was the target of the hostility. He must have wondered, Why was a man he had looked up to for so many years now coming at him with so much anger? I am sure he expected two seasoned pastors to discuss and transition through a dismissal without exposing him to so much hate and anger. But unfortunately, that did not happen.

It has often been said, "Hurting people hurt people." It was not THE MAN IN THE OFFICE NEXT DOOR's goal to cause my COF pain or to destroy the relationship. He was hurting! He was frustrated! He probably felt like he was placed on an island and was being blamed for the whole conflict. I am not sure why he reacted the way he did, nor why the emotions were directed to my CFO and not me. It doesn't matter; what does matter is that this would be the last time we would speak for six years.

OFFICE DOOR 2:

Blindsided. Shocked. Astonished. Dumbfounded. It's extremely rare that I'm ever caught off guard. However, I was on this day, February 14, 2013.

I was working part-time for two churches. I worked part-time at the church alongside THE MAN IN THE OFFICE NEXT DOOR and part-time for my spiritual father, as well. There were twenty-five miles between the two churches, but it always seemed like they were countries apart due to cultural differences.

One was an athletic town; the other was made up of simple, good ol' hardworking, men and women. I worked two days during the week at each location, alternated Sunday mornings, and oversaw the churches' youth ministries. One youth ministry met on Sunday evenings; the other met on Wednesday nights. One youth ministry was thriving; the other was in the early development stage. One youth ministry had a solid, equipped youth leadership team, while we were still sorting things out to see who we had to work with at the other.

The ministries were very diverse, and both brought my wife and me great joy. It was like teaching one of your kids to drive while teaching another to walk. Both were a bit scary, yet exciting nevertheless.

Things seemed to be going well with our ministries. We saw growth numerically and spiritually at both churches.

But then it happened.

It was a phone call I'll not soon forget. I was scheduled to be in the office at the church where my spiritual father pastored, but I received a phone call and was informed THE MAN IN THE OFFICE NEXT DOOR needed to meet with me instead. I remember thinking, Wow, that's odd; something must have happened down there, and we need an emergency meeting to discuss how we would resolve the issue.

I remember a conversation about the possibility of taking students on a mission trip soon, and I thought to myself, Maybe that's it. Maybe he wants to move forward with the idea and make it a reality. I drove down to the church and walked into THE MAN IN THE OFFICE NEXT DOOR's office to find him and his CFO waiting for me. They were both dressed in their Sunday best. That was a major red flag for me for a couple of reasons: 1) THE MAN IN THE OFFICE NEXT DOOR never dressed up during the workweek. 2) Our CFO was NEVER in the offices during the workweek, much less in business attire.

I walked into his office and said, "Wow, you guys are dressed up." I immediately thought to myself, You're dressed like you're going to a funeral. Little did I know they were, and it would be mine.

It was one of the most difficult meetings I have ever endured in my life. THE MAN IN THE OFFICE NEXT DOOR began the meeting by saying, "I'm going to get straight to the point. I don't know how else to say this, but..."

Stop!

Know this, if you are ever on the receiving end of that sentence, nothing that follows will be uplifting and encouraging.

As he began to speak the words, I could feel my blood pressure spike.

Back to the meeting. He said, "I'm going to get straight to the point. I don't know how else to say this, but as the Senior Pastor of this church, I cannot continue to allow what's been going on between us. I've consulted with a couple of men, and they agree, I'm going to have to let you go."

He used the passage of scripture in Acts 15, where Paul and Barnabas had a disagreement and parted ways. He just said it is what is best for this house, referring to the church. That was it. Short and sweet. Well, minus the sweet.

Nothing was said in the room for a couple of seconds. The silence seemed to last days. My thoughts began to go off like fireworks on the fourth of July. I sat in awe about what just happened.

Honestly, I think I was more upset about the choice of this day that he picked to let me go. IT WAS VALENTINE'S DAY, the day when you're supposed to get roses and candy, not roasted and canned!

All I could hear was my blood boiling from deep within my soul. It whistled like the Orient Express at top speed. Something had to give. I was about to.

All my life, I have felt "less than." All my life, people have told me what to do and ordered my steps for me. I have always taken pride in my work and honored the men and women in authority over me, to the best of my ability. I had never been fired in my life.

I finally spoke up and asked if this decision was based on a lack of finances. I knew our church was struggling a bit financially, and our lender had put a FOR SALE sign in front of our church weeks prior. I thought he might be downsizing and, if so, that would be an easier pill to swallow.

THE MAN IN THE OFFICE NEXT DOOR said it had nothing to do with finances. I asked if we could fix the situation, if we could fix us. I reminded him that we were family and friends before we were ever in ministry together. I suggested we seek outside help: someone, anyone, who wasn't privy to our situation and wouldn't be biased.

THE MAN IN THE OFFICE NEXT DOOR said that wasn't an option. He said we had gone too far, and the damage was done. He went on further to say, not only was I being released, but he said he needed my family and me to leave the church, as well. He said it would just be too much for our congregation to handle if my family and I stayed. He felt the division would only intensify.

I couldn't believe it. I was being fired for the first time in my life. I had never been cut from a basketball team, a football team, a wrestling team, nothing! I had quit many things I had started in life, but being cut or let go, never!

THE MAN IN THE OFFICE NEXT DOOR said something next that lit my fuse. He had ordered some lettering for one of our walls in the church. It was our church's mission statement and had been up for several months before this meeting. He said, "You don't even know our mission statement."

I quickly admitted, "No, I don't." And this would

prove to be the straw that broke the camel's back. I broke – or exploded. Erupted, I should say. I'm not sure exactly how to categorize it, but I did know this much, I had never in my life blown up on anyone the way I was about to.

I had looked at our CFO multiple times during the meeting as he sat with his head down, staring at the floor. Then it dawned on me: he was one of the men who suggested that I be let go. At least, that is what I heard in my mind. I felt like our CFO was integral to my termination. So, I went after him.

Every accusing thought I could think of came to my mind. I saw flashes of his sporadic church attendance. I caught glimpses of his absence from a couple of staff and support staff meetings. I unloaded on our CFO. I fired my first shot at him with an intense accusation, "You don't know the mission statement, either!"

It just came out without any resistance at all. And it felt good to accuse him, really good. I fired my second malicious shot, "Maybe we should fire you too!" I could sense the pleasure in my attempt to rip him apart. It was such a relief for me. I felt that if I was going out, I might as well go out with a bang. The bang was loud and on target.

I was hurt deeply. I felt betrayed and abandoned. I felt double-crossed and double-teamed. I was bleeding on the inside and wanted someone else to bleed, too. Somebody else in the room needed to bleed. They had to.

I knew my words had become weapons of mass destruction at this point, and I had every intention to fire at will.

LESSON LEARNED: An issue that is pushed under a rug and not dealt with will grow and gain strength until it comes out from under the rug and destroys everything it comes in contact with!

Deal with your differences head-on. It may be uncomfortable and seem like a dead-end road. You might be able to justify your innocence. However, you owe it to your future and to the people who are in your life to face the hard moments in life as they come instead of pushing them down further and further until you asphyxiate and die.

RYAN LUCIA (The CFO):

I had always known, while assisting with the business side of Covenant Connections Church, that the tension between Pastor David and Pastor Marty was high. I never wanted to get in the middle, so I tried to support both evenly. But my loyalty was with Pastor David for obvious reasons (if it's not obvious, he was my senior pastor).

Over the years, both would say things I felt should have been said to each other, but it appeared both had feelings that neither wanted to share with the other, resulting in even more division. I didn't feel as though I had the authority to try to intervene, first because it was a family matter and second, because both of them were people I genuinely looked up to and admired.

Pastor David asked if I would join him in a meeting with Pastor Marty to release him from his duties. This was the first time I think I've ever been genuinely frustrated with Pastor David. I understood why he asked; I just didn't think we had exhausted all opportunities, and I knew it wouldn't go well. I did it anyway because he asked.

The meeting didn't go well. At all! It was one of the worst meetings I've ever been a part of. I believe Pastor Marty felt ambushed and wondered why the heck I was even in the room. Pastor David almost seemed unemotional and determined to get through it. There were some cordial exchanges in which I interjected like a young, immature Christian in ministry would, sharing my infinite wisdom (kidding). That further upset Pastor Marty, and his anger and frustration towards the situation shifted to me.

As I sat there, I couldn't believe it. I love pastor Marty, and now I felt like he hated me. The truth is, the entire situation affected me more than just for that day. It's no secret that I'm not as involved in church ministry as I was. I believe it started here.

I had so much to say but couldn't pull the words. As a matter of fact, this is the first time I've even said anything about this outside of conversations with my wife. My wife has encouraged me to speak to Pastor David about this, but I never did.

After Pastor David and Marty reconciled, it was a huge relief for me. So much so that I drove to see Pastor Marty and apologized for speaking up in that meeting in an attempt to make things right. He was great about it, accepting my apology and speaking life into me exactly like the man I remembered before the confrontation.

I don't usually express my feelings, and when things

are bad, I typically avoid it if it only involves my feelings. I've had some resentment, and it's affected my decisions. A piece of my passion for the church and ministry left that day that has not yet returned.

When I was asked to share my experience for the book, I didn't want to. It's easier just to push the feelings down and walk away. Elder pastors are mentors and managers, and that's a challenging position, but the team that supports them may be in an even more difficult position. We can sometimes see things the leadership can't because we're close, but not too close. Being on the team, we see all the junk our pastor has to deal with, and your own stuff just doesn't seem important enough to cause more issues - sometimes, even at the cost of things becoming worse for yourself or the church. I view it as some sort of protection.

I see my faults. I knew I should speak up, but every time I attempted, I couldn't. Either the timing wasn't right, or I didn't know how to approach the situation. This went on for a while until I just decided that it had been a while, and it was not worth addressing anymore.

Family Crisis

You Can't Keep This in the House

OFFICE DOOR 2:

When you allow unresolved conflict to continue, chaos ensues. It will slowly eat away at relationships, ministries, churches, and families. It isn't biased one bit. Unresolved conflict is an Equal Opportunity Destroyer.

Unresolved conflict between me and THE MAN IN THE OFFICE NEXT DOOR had gotten so bad that it leaked into both of our families. Remember, he had married my first cousin. We weren't just in ministry together; we were family.

This unresolved conflict affected every church service, every church function, and now every family gathering. Birthdays wouldn't look the same. Holidays wouldn't look the same. Everything was stained at this point.

Every year, our families would get together at my Granny's house to celebrate Thanksgiving and Christmas. Inevitably, on Thanksgiving Day, my two daughters, all their cousins, and I would end up in

Granny's front yard playing football. It was a family tradition.

We made new memories each year. We had pictures to document those memories. Those pictures allowed us to go back year after year and remember the fun times our family had together. We played. We laughed. We poked fun at each other, and it was okay because we were family. We were strong together. We deeply loved each other. But those football games, the pictures, and the memory-making moments would cease. Things drastically changed within our extended family dynamic after the termination.

THE MAN IN THE OFFICE NEXT DOOR, his wife, and two children quit coming to our family Thanksgiving and Christmas gatherings. I remember, for the next year or two, my two girls would ask if we thought they would be able to see their two cousins at the particular gathering we were planning to attend. I would always respond, "Maybe. We will have to see." Deep down, I knew that we wouldn't be seeing them there.

At some point on the journey from our house to Granny's, I would look back in the rearview mirror time and time again to see my girls sitting silently in the back seat with tears streaming down their innocent, confused, wounded cheeks. We would end up asking if they were okay, and the girls would respond with things like, "I don't understand! What happened that was so bad that caused y'all not to get along anymore? Why can't y'all fix things and make it better? Can't we all just talk and work things out?"

My response was always, "I tried, but he fired me and asked us to leave his church."

Celebrating holidays and birthdays without their family would go on for years; six to be exact. No more football games. No more family memories. I was okay with that, and I wanted my family to be okay with that. Misery loves company.

And to think, what started with an annual holiday family football game in front of Granny's house, ended with a staff-versus-youth football game!

Over the next six years, I would watch his ministry grow. For six years, I heard how his church was thriving and how new ministries were birthed through his ministry. I couldn't stay in conversations very long when THE MAN IN THE OFFICE NEXT DOOR was mentioned.

Just that mention made my blood pressure rise immediately. It agitated me. I loved my cousin and her two children. I also loved him. I just didn't *like* him anymore. I came to a very dark place in my soul (my mind, will, and emotions) regarding THE MAN IN THE OFFICE NEXT DOOR. I realized that I had officially written him off. He was there, but he might as well have been make-believe. He F-I-R-E-D me! I had never been terminated from ANY position in my life! I didn't want to think about him anymore.

I removed his contact information from my phone. I unfriended and/or unfollowed him on all social media platforms. Any pictures I had stored on my phone of us, I deleted.

People would ask me from time to time, "Marty, does what happened between you guys feel like a divorce?"

My response was the same over the next six years: "No. It feels more like death."

OFFICE DOOR 1:

Unresolved conflict doesn't care who it destroys, as long as relationships die. Unresolved conflict doesn't have to have a title or recognition, nor does it have to be rewarded or celebrated. All unresolved conflict wants is a place to grow, fester, and breed, producing anger, hate, resentment, un-forgiveness, division, and, ultimately, death to any and every relationship.

I keep saying "unresolved conflict" because sometimes conflict is good for us as humans. When conflict is acknowledged, addressed, worked through, and ultimately resolved, it brings with it a lot of wisdom and experience.

Sometimes conflict can do more for your success than peace. Sometimes an enemy can do more for you than a friend. I heard a man say one time that Jesus rebuked Peter, who was his friend, and embraced Judas, who was his enemy. The reason why was that Peter was trying to keep Jesus from His destiny because he loved Him and didn't want Jesus to have to die for humanity. So Peter, Jesus' friend, actually became a stumbling block to Jesus.

Judas, however, became useful to Jesus at that moment because he was helping Jesus achieve His ultimate destiny. Sometimes we must embrace our conflict and resist the times of peace and tranquility. Whatever we do, we cannot allow conflict to go unresolved!

The unresolved conflict between THE MAN IN THE OFFICE NEXT DOOR and me had reached such a fevered pitch that even our families had to choose a side. Remember, THE MAN IN THE OFFICE NEXT DOOR was my wife's first cousin. Not only that, but he was also one of her very favorite cousins. Their mothers were sisters.

My own family was not very close for many years. My dad had passed away in 1998. My mother and stepfather traveled all over the country for his job. He was a general contractor supervisor. So wherever the next job was, they had to be on-site for many months at a time, requiring them to move all over the country. My siblings had their own families and responsibilities, so we didn't spend many holidays and special events together. We would always spend these times with THE MAN IN THE OFFICE NEXT DOOR, his family, and extended family.

Every Christmas, my children had always played in the yard with their cousins. THE MAN IN THE OFFICE NEXT DOOR would play football with all the cousins every Christmas morning. I would sit on the sidelines and watch. Sometimes I would have to retrieve a ball out of a bush or one that rolled into the side street.

My kids could hardly wait for special events or holidays so they could have time with family. There was no question about what we were doing every Christmas, Thanksgiving, most birthdays, and other planned family events. We would be at Granny's house playing football in the front yard, eating home-cooked food, and playing around the old piano that only had three or four keys that even made a noise. That piano was so old most of the keys had no spring to them. They just played flat on the piano face. But the kids would beat and bang on it, wearing out the three or four keys that still made some kind of noise. Every holiday, every special event, our families were together.

I remember the first holiday after the dismissal.

My children, who were nine and twelve at the time, asked my wife and me the night before, "Are we going to spend time with the family?" You see, it was the only family they knew, the only grandparents that brought even a little stability to their lives. The cousins were the only cousins they spent real time with. The aunts and uncles were the only ones they knew by name and had memories with at that time.

My children were not mixed up in the conflict. My wife and I did a pretty good job of protecting our kids from the horrors of dealing with people. All our children knew was that they wanted to see their cousins, play football, hug their aunts and uncles, and beat the old piano keys. Of course, they did care that adults were acting like babies, and they knew that conflict had given birth to a war that would separate even the closest of families. They just really wanted to do what they had done their whole lives.

I remember telling them that we would not be going to family events anymore. As I look back now, I can't help but remember the confusion on their little faces, the pain in their adolescent eyes. As their parents, we drew a line of separation and the kids had no choice as to which side they would take. We had made the choice for them.

There is an old saying, "What goes on in this house stays in this house." Well, some things you just can't keep in the house.

Unresolved conflict is one of those things. It will fester until it becomes like leaven and pollute everything it contacts. The leaven of un-forgiveness had poisoned our whole family.

For years, we stayed home for Christmas. No front yard football at Thanksgiving. Birthdays were celebrated only in our immediate family and a few of our children's friends. For several months, when big events or holidays would come around, my wife and I would prepare ourselves for the question, "Are we going to the family event?" Our answer would always be the same, "Not this time."

It wasn't long before the questions ceased. Everyone just knew we stood on different sides of the line.

Each side stood with swords in hand, bloody from the battle, tired and weary, but neither side was willing to admit defeat.

It was inevitable that what began at a flag football game had now ended in a family crisis.

LESSON LEARNED: Conflict that goes unresolved hibernates in the cave of selfishness. Oftentimes, we become so focused on our own feelings and emotions that we forget there are so many others intertwined in our decisions. Don't let selfishness draw others to the lines you have drawn in the sand, requiring them to choose sides as well. *"Dont let the sun go down on your wrath."* (Ephsians 4:26)

The Revival Service

The Power of Repentance and Forgiveness

OFFICE DOOR 1:

Something huge happened about six years after the dismissal.

My pastor was serving a church approximately thirty miles north of where I lived. In January of that year, he called his church to observe a twenty-one-day fast with prayer to begin the new year.

This was not uncommon at all in our region of the world. Many churches, families, or groups would begin their new year with a time of fasting and prayer. However, those twenty-one days were to signal a significant move of God for my pastor's congregation, and even for thousands far beyond our region.

During what began as a routine Bible college class held at my pastor's church, the Spirit of the Lord came into the room where a small group of dedicated men and women were in attendance. Later reports revealed that the event was not an extravagant display of God's presence; He just "sat down" in the room, they said. There were no fiery manifestations, no loud proclamations of His arrival, and no angelic hosts knocking over tables to declare His entrance. There was just the sweet, quiet presence of God filling the people.

Everyone in the room testified of experiencing His entrance. Most of them just began to weep, some began worshiping, but all became reverently attentive. Then just as quickly as He came, He left.

Little did anyone know that this would be the beginning of one of the greatest revivals of our time.

Later in the twenty-one-day fast, during personal prayer time, my pastor was given a vision of fire on top of water in the baptistry located inside the church's main auditorium. The baptistry was empty, and no one was in the sanctuary except the pastor.

He is not a man who has frequent spiritual dreams or open visions, but the vision was clear on this day. He saw the baptistry full of water and flame of fire approximately two to three feet wide stitching from the front to the back of the baptismal pool.

As he pondered what he was seeing, the Spirit of the Lord spoke to him and said, "I will baptize my people with Holy Spirit Fire."

In response to what the pastor believed the Lord desired, he met with several local pastors to relate the experience and discuss holding revival meetings. Not long afterward, several churches began to meet every Sunday night for revival services. During these services, we would experience incredible moments of worship. There would be hundreds, and even, at times, over a thousand people gather to experience the presence of God and to be baptized.

Hundreds and hundreds of salvations were occurring during the revival services. We couldn't document the miracles that God began doing in the baptismal waters of the revival. You name it; God did it.

Marriages were restored, diseases were cured, and families were brought back together. The Word of God was preached in power and demonstration. Thousands of individuals were baptized with Holy Spirit fire during the revival services.

Early on in the revival, my pastor reached out to me about coming and attending the revival services. I wanted to go. I wanted more of God. I wanted to be a part of what God was doing. But THE MAN IN THE OFFICE NEXT DOOR was now the youth pastor and executive pastor of the church where the revival was taking place. Not only that, but dozens of people who used to go to my church were now attending, serving in, and even leading the revival services there.

You talk about emotional and spiritual overload! My mind and my emotions were all over the map. I kept telling my pastor that I would come, but for weeks I had something else I just *HAD* to do.

One day, my pastor called me and asked me to come the following Sunday night. He said, "Give me your word you will come." He knew if I made a commitment, I would do what I said. So I told him I would come to the revival meeting. I remember I was miserable for days. Leading up to my arrival at the church, I was almost physically sick. I knew there would be a large group of people attending the meeting that hated me. I knew they didn't want to see me, and I didn't care to see or speak to them, either.

I took one of my elders with me, and we arrived just a few minutes late for the service – just late enough to walk in and grab a seat in the very back. I had asked my pastor NOT to acknowledge that I was there. I wanted to fulfill my commitment and attend the service by sneaking in and sneaking out.

Well, that didn't happen. Upon entering the building, the first people I encountered were a couple who had left my church to attend this church. It wasn't a bad encounter because the couple lived about forty minutes away from our church, and this church was five miles from their house. Nevertheless, it was still a loss for me.

As I walked through the foyer, I recognized a man walking towards me but couldn't quite recall who he was. As my mind went a hundred miles an hour trying to think of who this person was, I remembered: he and his family attended our church for several weeks, came to one of our New Covenant Partners Luncheons (new-members' luncheon), and actually joined the church. Then they never came back. With a huge smile on his face, he reached for my hand as though to welcome me to his new church home. I reluctantly shook his hand and continued to make my way into the service.

I tried to sneak into the sanctuary; it was so dark I couldn't see my hand in front of my face. As I walked cautiously forward, looking for a seat in the very back, I was grabbed and bear-hugged by someone or something! If you know me, you know I like my own space. I don't like being bumped or grabbed by surprise. Not only was I already in a very uncomfortable situation and unable to see my surroundings, now I was being grabbed by someone!

As I was finally able to adjust my eyes to see who or what had a hold on me, I realized it was a man who had just left my church a few weeks before to attend this church. Even worse, he had attended my church for years, and when He left, he never even told me he was going. I found out through mutual friends that he was attending my pastor's church.

I am not making this stuff up! It is so true!

As soon as he let me go, I was immediately confronted by another man coming to shake my hand. When I saw this man, I half-heartedly accepted his handshake, making it a quick one. I didn't want him to think I liked him overly much.

Why? This man also had left my church without even letting me know. He was there one Sunday and gone the next, never to return. There had been no explanation, no conversation, no good-bye – he was just gone. More than that, he had been a hunting buddy of mine. We were friends outside of a pastoral relationship. So, not only did I lose a church member, I lost a friend. With no explanation!

I had not been on the campus five minutes, and I had run into one couple and two individuals about whom I was carrying – at the least – a feeling of rejection and loss. Everything I was afraid of happening was happening before I even found a back-row seat!

My elder and I found seats right beside the back doors. We even sat at the end of the row so that, as soon as the speaker began to close his message in prayer, we could sneak out.

As we sat there and I inconspicuously examined the crowd, I saw person after person that had left my life because of the conflict between me and THE MAN IN THE OFFICE NEXT DOOR. They had chosen him over me. They had chosen his truth over my truth. His perspective was the side of the line they willingly stood on while rejecting my viewpoint. These were the thoughts that were crashing in my mind like the waves of a typhoon.

I almost bailed out of the situation. I became physically sick. All the rejection I had experienced as a child, a teenager, and now, as an adult, was kicking my rear end to the point I looked at my elder and said, "I don't know if I can stay."

Everything in me told me to run out of the sanctuary doors, get in my truck, and get back to my safe environment. By God's grace, I mustered enough strength to stay seated, telling myself all I had to do was sit there until the end of the service when I could bolt unnoticed. That is, until THE ACKNOWLEDGMENT.

My pastor decided to disregard my request not to acknowledge my presence in the room. From the stage, while he spoke into *a very loud microphone*, he not only acknowledged that I was in attendance, he then asked me to stand.

My thought was, "Oh my Lord Jesus, please help me!"

I stood but not much more than a shallow bend. I threw my hand up and mustered a slight grin. Then I sat back down quickly.

What just happened, I thought. I asked my pastor

NOT to acknowledge me. Was he being mean! Was he agitating the situation? Was he disrespecting me and my request?

My running shoes were on, warmed up, and ready to hit the carpet, but something in me kept me in place. I stayed, though I could not tell you one thing the speaker said. I couldn't tell you one song the praise and worship team sang. (Of course, the praise and worship team consisted of nine people, six of whom had been members of my church, and who left with THE MAN FROM THE OFFICE NEXT DOOR – including the worship leaders, who had been on my staff before the dismissal.)

Before the preacher could say "Amen!" to his closing prayer, my elder and I were out of that place and driving home. I thought to myself, I will NEVER go back to that revival!

A couple of days later, my pastor and his wife came to watch my son play basketball. This is something we had in common because their youngest son played basketball in college, and my son was a great player as well.

After the game was over, we began to talk about what God was doing at the North Georgia Revival. I could feel the question coming afar off. I tried to end the conversation or derail the topic before he could ask the question, but it was as though my pastor knew what I was doing and was one step ahead of me.

When there was a slight pause in the conversation, out came the question.

"Will you check your calendar and come minister at the revival?" he asked.

"Pastor," I answered cautiously. "I love you, and I know you love me. You know I will do anything you ask me to do. But, you don't want me to come to preach at your revival. There are people there that hate me, and they don't want to hear anything I have to say. I don't want to interfere with what Holy Spirit is doing at the revival."

His reply to me was as though he had not even heard my excuse. He said he would call me the next week, and we would come up with a date for me to minister there.

My immediate thought was, "Okay, whatever!"

I didn't expect him to call. But he did. Amazingly, we agreed on a date.

I remember ministering the first time I preached at the revival. The Lord was so gracious and merciful. The Spirit of the Lord moved in a great way. Despite all the anger, un-forgiveness, bitterness, and resentment in the room, He moved! It was like I was in a bubble of God's presence.

As I preached, I couldn't see faces in the congregation. It was like I looked right past the people and saw the reason I was there: that God wanted me to be who He created me to be and to present Him to the people.

The night was great! But still, as soon as I could sneak out, my family and I were out of there!

However, something happened that made me step back and think a little. My son and daughter came to me just before we left and asked if they could get a bite to eat with THE MAN IN THE OFFICE NEXT DOOR's daughters along with the sons of a lady who was my wife's best friend before the dismissal.

I didn't know how to feel. My first reaction to them was to say, No! You are on this side of the line, and they are still on the other. At the same time, my first emotion was that familiar voice of rejection because now my children seemed to be choosing the other side over me. Maybe because I was still under the anointing of God, or perhaps because, deep down inside, I was ready for this all to be over, I said, "Sure, you can go eat with them. Just be safe, and we will see you at home."

This was just the first of serval times I would minister during the revival in North Georgia. Not only that, but my pastor asked me to be one of the selected pastors who would help him lead the revival and offer him counsel concerning the move of God.

I felt honored to say yes. It was the beginning of a significant restoration in my life. But guess who else was on Pastor's counsel?

Yep, THE MAN IN THE OFFICE NEXT DOOR. It had been years since we spoke. Our paths had only crossed very few times, at a funeral here or there, or maybe at a graduation service or ball game. At those times, we would just turn our heads or look at the ground until one or the other had passed. But now we would be stuck in closed-door meetings with other pastors.

I figured we could just pretend the other guy was not in the room. We might even be able to speak civilly to each other if we were put on the spot. But other than that, we could maintain our distance and not even need to look at each other.

That was, until January 13th, 2019!

That service in January was the event God had been orchestrating for months. I was scheduled to minister at the North Georgia Revival that evening. I was ready! The Lord had been dealing with me for several weeks about repenting to THE MAN IN THE OFFICE NEXT DOOR, his family, and anyone else I could pour my heart out to. You see, I was tired! I was tired of carrying all these emotions. I was tired of trying to lead people to a place of repentance where I wasn't willing to go. I couldn't live this way anymore. I knew that we had lost a lot of years hiding behind our conflict. I just couldn't live out of this pain any longer!

One Sunday morning, I felt in my heart that I needed to send a text to THE MAN IN THE OFFICE NEXT DOOR, asking him to forgive me. I made it clear I would one day repent to him face to face. I just had to release this conflict. I had to get it off of me as soon as I could.

Earlier in the week, as I prayed at my church, the Lord began to speak to my heart a revelation of His Word concerning the restoration between everyone involved in the conflict. So I went into the revival service knowing that God wanted to bring healing to us all. I was still a little uneasy about how THE MAN IN THE OFFICE NEXT DOOR and others involved would react. I wasn't sure if I would be rejected or embraced. But their reaction didn't matter to me. I knew I had heard from the Lord, and I HAD to be healed!

I felt it was as though we were living out the Genesis story of the elderly Isaac calling Esau to himself to pass on the blessing of the first-born son. Scripture tells us that Isaac's eyes were dim, and he was about to die. He was about to receive his eternal reward, and all he had to do first was pass blessings to his sons.

The blessing was to go to the eldest son first. So Isaac called Esau to his bedside. However, Isaac's wife, knowing what was about to happen, wanted the younger son, Jacob, to receive the blessing. The story goes that she devised a plan for Jacob to receive the blessing instead of Esau. The plan worked, and Jacob stole Esau's blessing. This created immediate conflict between the brothers, so much so that Esau wanted to take Jacob's life. As a result, Jacob ran away in fear.

Over the next several chapters, the Bible tells us of Jacob's life and a little about Esau's. But it climaxes when Jacob returns to the land God wanted to give him, and Esau was coming to find Jacob. They had been in conflict for decades without any communication. They met on the banks of a river, and, as the story goes, they forgave each other. They embraced each other, and so their families were united.

In Genesis chapter 35, we read that they went to see their father, Isaac, in all probability to let him know the conflict was over. The events between chapter 28 and chapter 35 took place over a 43 to 46 year period. That means that Isaac, who had been ready to die and receive his eternal reward, lived another 43 to 46 years to see the conflict resolved that hit his home and divided his sons.

The Lord showed me that neither my pastor, THE MAN IN THE OFFICE NEXT DOOR, nor I could move into our full reward or destiny until the conflict was resolved.

Well, that night, at the end of my message, I invited THE MAN IN THE OFFICE NEXT DOOR to join me on stage. I told him, our pastor, and the whole congregation what the Lord had shown me. I repented to him and asked for his forgiveness. We embraced for what seemed to be several minutes as we both repented to and forgave each other.

He asked if he could hug my wife. She walked up the stairs of the platform, sobbing almost uncontrollably. Then we were joined by THE MAN IN THE OFFICE NEXT DOOR's wife and his two daughters. After that, my son and daughter came onto the stage, as well. Years of pain, flowing down our faces in the form of tears, disappeared as we all embraced. Heartache was mended in a moment. Years of separation were restored in an instant. No words needed to be spoken. The repentance was absolute, and the forgiveness was evident.

That revival service gave way to a chain of events that would last weeks and months in our lives and the lives of those attending the service. Emotional healing was released in that atmosphere in a way I have never see. I still hear stories of people who were in that revival service or who watched the video of the service online, stories of how others were moved to repent to someone or how they had to forgive someone.

The cycle had been broken! The conflict that had spanned more than eight years ended in one act of humility. There is nothing more potent than the power of repentance and forgiveness!

Our whole eternity hinges on these two things: the

willingness to repent when we are wrong and the ability to forgive when others request it from us.

This was the most powerful service I have ever been involved with in my life. No fancy building, no well-known preacher, no counseling session. Just a moment in time when God took the stage and said, "Now it's time for Me to be glorified!"

OFFICE DOOR 2:

Six years have passed. Six long years. On the outside, life was good. Family bonds were sound. Ministry was effective. But, inside, I was frustrated, broken, miserable, and feeling more and more like a hypocrite by the day for the fact that I could preach forgiveness but not live it.

I was on full-time staff with my spiritual parents in Dawsonville, GA. The year was 2018. My pastor had called the church to twenty-one days of prayer and fasting. This was the typical way for churches to begin a new year.

However, this year's fast would prove to be anything but ordinary.

Our pastor felt the leading of Holy Spirit to ask our congregation to agree with and join him in praying and fasting for three specific things: (1) that we, as a congregation, would seek God's face; (2) that we would behold His beauty and His glory; and (3) that the Lord would press in to us.

He felt that this year we should pray and seek the Lord's face versus what was in His hand.

On one occasion, during his prayer time, my pastor

received an open vision from the Lord. He had never had an open vision before this one. Alone in prayer, walking across the platform in our main sanctuary, his attention was drawn toward the baptismal pool. Although it was empty, naturally speaking, in the spirit, he saw the pool full of water, and a strip of fire ran over the surface (as though someone had poured gasoline on top of the water and lit it).

At that moment, the Lord spoke to him: "I am going to baptize my people with Holy Spirit fire." He did not fully understand what that meant, nor would he, until months later.

Soon after that vision, the presence of the Lord began to show up in our meetings in a new, fresh, powerful way. And as we recognized we were in revival, the pastors of four or five churches in our area began to host revival services at our church. The Lord began to heal people in the baptismal waters here. Many were experiencing the power of God during worship. And many more were moved spontaneously to be baptized in the waters.

The occurrence of healings and miracles increased. It was beautiful. Weeks into the meetings, hundreds upon hundreds were showing up every Sunday night from all over the country and the world to experience the presence of God and to be baptized in the water at our church.

Countless people have given their lives to the Lord during this revival. Although we attempted to document every miracle that the Lord did in the water, they began to be so frequent we could not keep count. They increased exponentially. We simply could not record every single one.

Marriages were restored. The sick were healed. Families were fortified. So many were baptized with Holy Spirit fire during the revival services that we would baptize all evening and into the early morning hours. I loved it. I loved being in the water with people from around the globe, coming to meet with Jesus in the water. I witnessed amazing miracles in the water: the toughest of men weeping and being broken in His presence. Being in the baptism water at the North Georgia Revival is an incomparable experience, and it's difficult to imagine more of heaven on earth than that.

Being so caught up in the revival experience, I was not expecting what happened next. I didn't see it coming at all.

One evening, as my pastor got up to transition the service, receive the offering and turn it over to our guest speaker, he stopped the service to recognize someone special who was sitting out in the congregation. I could not believe it. After dodging THE MAN IN THE OFFICE NEXT DOOR pretty well for six years, I suddenly could not avoid it. He was sitting in the audience. My pastor asked him to stand, and he began to celebrate and honor him in front of seven hundred or more people in attendance that night.

Almost everyone applauded. Not only did I NOT applaud, but I was also appalled. How could he? How dare he step on MY turf! He had his own church! Why was he coming here? Why was my pastor acknowledging him when he knew full well the toxic feelings we had toward each other? I was fuming mad. Somehow I endured the service.

When the preacher finished his message, it was time for baptisms. I got in the water as I had done the previous weeks. Only this time, I found myself surveying the audience to see if THE MAN IN THE OFFICE NEXT DOOR was still in the building. I did not want him to be there. From what I could tell, he wasn't. Everything was okay. I could breathe more freely now and focus on the task at hand, having safely dodged a close encounter.

Several weeks later, in a staff meeting, we were discussing the revival, giving praise reports, and my pastor wanted to review the speaking schedule for the upcoming weeks. What he said next shook me to my core. He had invited THE MAN IN THE OFFICE NEXT DOOR to come and preach a night of the revival! And he had accepted!

I felt my ears getting hot. Sweat began to gather in my palms. Simultaneously, all eyes in the room riveted on me. At least it felt that way.

You've got to be joking me! I thought to myself. This is not happening, right? This has to be a bad dream. I thought, "Why am I still sitting here? I should resign right now! This is absurd!"

Well, I didn't quit

And he did come to preach.

(Actually, I found out later that, after the service, my children and his children went out to eat while I was in the water baptizing people, and after THE MAN IN THE OFFICE NEXT DOOR had already gone home. Our kids were getting together for the first time in six years! That was huge!)

The message he preached that night was powerful. He

always had preached powerfully and with such authority and boldness. And he had always seen powerful response to every altar call he gave. He's always been so anointed to preach and prophesy and pray!

Maybe that was one reason I didn't like him any longer; he was more gifted in that area than I was. Maybe I was jealous, and that was what put me on edge around him.

As I began meditating on those thoughts, the Lord started showing me that something wasn't wrong with him; something was wrong in me.

Anyway, I was very glad the night was over. I comforted myself with the thought that maybe he would not be invited back. I couldn't handle it. It was too much. He and I in the same room? It was not good.

Well, it was good for my pastor. He not only invited him to come to preach again at the revival but now I found out my pastor has asked THE MAN IN THE OFFICE NEXT DOOR to be one of the host pastors! He was about to help lead the revival from this point forward!

The host pastors met consistently to help facilitate the many details of the revival. Guess who else sat in on these meetings? Me! Being in an auditorium with him along with nearly a thousand others is one thing; sitting in a conference room with him and five or six other pastors is an entirely different story.

We hadn't spoken to each other in years, mind you. And now we were expected to sit mere feet apart in a small meeting space.

As it turned out, we sat in those meetings numerous times without saying anything at all to each other, unless we just had to. It was terrible. It was torture.

The next time THE MAN IN THE OFFICE NEXT DOOR was scheduled to preach, it was in the fall of 2018. On this particular night, I had already changed my clothes and was in the baptistry, praying and preparing to receive the first baptismal candidates of the evening.

As I came out to the front of the baptismal pool where my microphone and towels were, I took the mic in my hand and was ready for the first candidate to come and be immersed. To my amazement, one of the first ones to come around the corner was, wait for it – yep, it was THE MAN IN THE OFFICE NEXT DOOR.

Following his sermon, my pastor asked him to assist with water baptisms for a while that evening. It was one of the most awkward moments of my life. I'm sure he felt the same. We hadn't spoken in years. We dodged each other in public. Yet, here we stood, ministering together in water baptisms.

Several candidates had come through, and everything went as usual until we had a gentleman that came up out of the water and began thrashing around with his arms and legs going everywhere. Well, as you can imagine, water was going everywhere too. He was splashing water over every single one of our volunteers, THE MAN IN THE OFFICE NEXT DOOR, and me. Even those standing around the outside of the pool watching the baptisms were getting wet. This went on for what seemed like minutes. I'm sure it was only fifteen or twenty seconds or so, but it seemed like forever.

Once everything calmed down, and our volunteers assisted the candidate to the steps, I grabbed my towel and began to dry my hands, arms, face, and head. After I was somewhat dry, I placed the towel back on the baptismal pool's outer edge and turned to see THE MAN IN THE OFFICE NEXT DOOR attempting to dry his wet face with his wet arms and hands. He wasn't getting much accomplished. My initial thought – a very spiritual one – was, "Oh wow! He doesn't have a towel to dry off with." My second thought – a very UN-spiritual one – was, "Oh well, he's a grown man; he will figure it out."

I know! I know! Here I am being used by the Lord in one of the greatest awakenings and revivals the world has ever seen, and I am having thoughts like these!

I get it!

That's just where I was: bitter and offended. I was hurt. I am just being transparent and honest.

It's a wonder the Lord didn't strike me dead for my thoughts. I was sure the Lord was upset with me and wouldn't speak to me any longer. Boy, was I wrong!

As soon as I had those thoughts, the Lord spoke to me. I didn't hear it audibly, but I knew deep down in my spirit that it was Him.

He said, "Marty, get him a towel."

That's one of the reasons I knew it was the Lord. I would never in a million years have thought to get him a towel. My thoughts were more along the lines of, "He can get his own towel."

But the Lord must have heard my thought because He fired right back with, "Yes, he can get his own towel.

Or you could get it for him."

So I rebutted with, "I could, Lord, but I don't want to."

The Lord gently, softly, replied, "I know you don't want to. That's why I suggested it."

Here I am trying to have a debate with the Creator of the universe! Needless to say, it's always a good thing to be obedient to what the Lord asks of you.

I turned to one of our volunteers and asked for another towel. When I had it, I turned to THE MAN IN THE OFFICE NEXT DOOR, got his attention, and offered him the towel. He accepted it.

The instant his hand touched the towel, something happened. The only way I can put it into words is, it was like an atomic bomb exploded on the inside of me, and I heard the words, "It's done."

Now, I didn't receive those words as if the Lord had erased every hurt, every ounce of pain or that He had wiped all the bitterness away. I received them as the Lord had set something in motion through that one simple act of obedience, and that it would eventually lead to the restoration of our relationship. It was just a matter of time now.

Fast forward several months to January 2019. I needed a break, just to breathe some fresh air for a while. My pastor asked my wife and me to go with them on a ministry trip to Moody, Alabama. He had been asked to share what the Lord was doing in the Dawsonville revival services.

Paula and I decided to go with them. It would be refreshing for us since we wouldn't have to do anything. I was used to helping host hundreds each week at our services, answering tons of phone calls about the revival, and responding to as many emails.

On this trip, I wouldn't have to do anything. My pastor was scheduled to speak on that Saturday morning, but we went over on Friday to attend an evening service at the church.

The praise and worship were amazing that night. The preacher who brought the message – Pastor Johnny Taylor – was my kind of preacher: extremely passionate, biblically sound, and authentic. He wept. A lot. And I was so into his message that I was sitting on the edge of my seat.

My wife and I were seated near the front row's end seat, next to my pastor and his wife. Pastor Johnny was across the sanctuary preaching up a storm when he suddenly stopped and whipped his head around. He stared right at me. Then he ran across the front of the church and stopped directly in front of me.

I had never met this man before in my life. He asked me to stand up. I stood, and he began looking deeply into my eyes. His eyes were piercing, as if he was looking straight through me and into my soul. He began to weep as he spoke to me. Moving his left hand in a karate-chop motion, he started hitting my chest while repeating these four words: "Like it never happened! Like it never happened! Like it never happened!"

The Lord gave Pastor Johnny a word of knowledge for me.

For those who may not understand what a word of knowledge is, it is a spiritual gift found in the Bible in

1 Corinthians 12:8. The word of knowledge is simply the Holy Spirit transmitting His specific knowledge to you about someone or something that you or the person speaking would have no ability or means to know otherwise. It is supernatural knowledge and insight given directly to someone about another person or thing by Holy Spirit Himself. It isn't a thought or idea, intelligence or knowledge attained elsewhere.

The word of knowledge Pastor Johnny spoke to me that night was so profound and so precise, I knew immediately and exactly what he meant when he said, "Like it never happened!"

The next Sunday evening, January 13, 2019, at the North Georgia Revival, THE MAN IN THE OFFICE NEXT DOOR just so happened to be scheduled to preach again. While he was speaking, near the time for the altar call, I slipped out the back of the sanctuary and headed straight for the room where I usually change into my baptism clothes. I entered the room, put my phone on silent, and placed it on the bathroom counter as I began changing my clothes.

It was the same routine week after week. I would always drink a sixteen-ounce bottle of water and eat one of my protein bars to boost my energy because I never knew how long I would be in the water.

As I finished changing, I noticed my phone was lit. I grabbed it and noticed I had several missed calls and numerous texts from my daughters and my wife. On calling my wife, she immediately answered the phone and asked, "Where are you?"

I replied, "Babe, I'm in the same place I always am at this time on Sunday evenings. Is everything okay?"

As soon as I asked that, there was a hard, stern knock on the bathroom door. I opened the door to find a gentleman in seeming terror as if he had seen a ghost. He was as pale as a sheet.

He informed me that THE MAN IN THE OFFICE NEXT DOOR was calling for me to come to the stage.

"What are you talking about?" I asked.

"You are needed on the stage, sir."

The bathroom was only a few steps to the ministry stage, so I went up a short flight of stairs, turned the corner, and came out from behind our stage backdrop onto the stage. There he was, calling for me. As far as I can remember, only the two of us were on the stage. In the congregation were several hundred people in attendance. Hundreds more – maybe thousands – watched LIVE on Facebook, on our YouTube channel, or on Sid Roth's *It's Supernatural Network* (ISN).

THE MAN IN THE OFFICE NEXT DOOR began to address me directly. I moved closer until we stood face to face.

Suddenly, he began to repent in front of everyone. He began to weep. I sensed raw, authentic repentance from him.

He apologized for the way he handled things six years before. He asked for my forgiveness. I forgave him.

I genuinely and thoroughly forgave him. It was so freeing. I felt so light. I didn't feel like I was in a dream. I knew it was real.

After a moment, I asked him if it would be okay to invite my cousin – his wife – on stage and for me repent to her, as well. He agreed. (Why did I do this?

Because I believe honor is the antidote to hurt, to bitterness, un-forgiveness, and division.)

The next thing I knew, my wife and two daughters were on the stage, his wife and children were on the stage, and we were all broken and weeping. It was unlike any service I had ever experienced in my life.

I'm not exactly sure who to give credit to, but someone more intelligent and experienced than I once said, "To forgive is to set a person free, and then discover that person was you."

LESSON LEARNED: Ecclesiastes 4:12 says *"And if one prevail against him, two shall withstand him; and a <u>threefold cord is not quickly broken</u>."*

There is nothing more powerful than the three-fold cord plaited with Love, Repentance, and Forgiveness. The whole Gospel is summed up in these three words. You can't have the Gospel of Jesus without these three words. Neither can you live in peace, joy, and success without these three words! Seek them out, choose them, and never let them escape your grasp.

Like It Never Happened!

The Baptism

OFFICE DOOR 2:

It came to pass.

The word the Lord gave me in the water in the fall of 2018, when He asked me to get THE MAN IN THE OFFICE NEXT DOOR a towel, was "I'm going to restore everything."

And, on this day – January 13, 2019, around 7:30 pm – it came to pass.

Johnny Taylor's word of knowledge from a week prior came to fruition.

Broken and obliterated were nearly six years of unforgiveness. Seventy-one months! Three-hundred-eight weeks and three days! Two thousand, one hundred fifty-nine days total! Five years, ten months, thirty days! 51,816 hours! 3,108,960 seconds!

But who's counting, right?

What a night! But just when I thought things couldn't possibly get any better, we moved from the stage to the baptismal pool.

THE MAN IN THE OFFICE NEXT DOOR and his wife were the first ones to enter the water. I took the microphone just like I had done for the past fifty weeks or so. I would typically begin the baptism interview with the candidate or candidates by asking a series of questions: 1) What is your name? 2) Where are you from? 3) Why are you in the water? 4) Do you want to hold your nose?

Tonight would begin a bit differently. I began to repent to THE MAN IN THE OFFICE NEXT DOOR and his wife, my cousin, for the things that had transpired over the last six years. I repented openly, authentically, publicly.

Jesus modeled true forgiveness openly and publicly. It was our model. Suspended on an old rugged cross between heaven and Earth, Jesus hung stripped, nearly naked, in front of His accusers who had beaten Him as close to death as one could come. Yet, He looked up toward the heavens and said, *"Father, forgive them, for they know not what they do."*

I asked both of them to forgive me, and they did. Before I knew it, I was speaking – NO, declaring – these words over us, "Like it never happened!"

When I released those words, I believe in that exact moment, the Father released His forgiveness over the two of them, over me, over us, over the situation, over our families, over our ministries, and anything else connected to us.

I was ready to baptize the two of them, when all of a sudden, my pastor - *our* pastor - climbed over the wall and glass of the baptistry and got down into the water, fully clothed with what he wore to church that night, eyeglasses and all.

The place was shaken.

You could hear the roar of hundreds as they shouted

in approval. You could see grown men and women crying uncontrollably. Freedom entered the room.

It was as though angels filled the atmosphere in approval of what was happening.

Our pastor pulled his glasses off and locked arms with me and THE MAN IN THE OFFICE NEXT DOOR. He whispered, "Baptize all three of us together." It was as if, at that moment, we could sense years upon years of pain, anger, frustration, and offense were about to melt. The weight of six years of people's prayers and intercession for us had sat down on us at that moment.

Three men who had served in ministry together for decades, who had traveled the world together, yet who had distance between them due to conflict, were about to be restored like never before. We had all witnessed thousands upon thousands of others go down into this watery grave and experience healing and deliverance. We knew we would encounter the same and more.

Down the three of us went into the healing, restoring waters at the North Georgia Revival. The men God chose to help lead this move of God had been led by the Lord down into the water themselves to encounter healing, as well.

It was powerful, beautiful, and so relieving. It brought healing and joy. Such a wonderful experience! Chains fell off. Anger left. Years and years of silence and pain were broken. Heartache was healed. Walls came down.

So did His presence also come down, His power and His glory. Jesus made it LIKE IT NEVER

HAPPENED!

OFFICE DOOR 1:

I can't help but think of the old spiritual that says, "Wade in the water; wade in the water, children. Wade in the water, for God's going to trouble the water." That hymn was sung by freed slaves throughout the underground railroad to lead the other slaves to freedom.

The night THE MAN IN THE OFFICE NEXT DOOR, my wife, and I stood in the baptistry at the North Georgia Revival was a visual of this song. Three spiritually-bound slaves were being led to freedom through the waters of baptism. We were bound by unforgiveness, years of rejection, and all the other emotions that bind us to our lack of repentance.

But this was the night our victory would manifest. There was nothing special about the water that filled the baptismal pool that night. There was no miracle anointing oil poured into the baptistry. The main things that entered the baptistry that night were humility, obedience, and love. Humility will always attract God's presence. Obedience will always attract the miraculous. Love will always produce an atmosphere where healing and restoration will prevail and deliver.

THE MAN IN THE OFFICE NEXT DOOR took the microphone to do what he routinely did before baptizing anyone. He would ask their names and why they were in the water that evening. Often, he would give the candidate an inspiring word of encouragement or, at times, a direct word from the

Lord. At this time, THE MAN IN THE OFFICE NEXT DOOR took time to publicly repent to my wife and me before the hundreds of people attending the revival and many more watching the live stream over the Internet.

We have to understand that true repentance is always an open event. Real repentance must not stay behind closed doors. Repentance and forgiveness were displayed on Calvary's Hill over two thousand years ago. I am referring to the time an innocent Man was suspended from a convict's cross. As He fought for each breath, Jesus had enough strength to declare these words, *"Father forgive them for they know not what they do."*

This is the process for repentance and forgiveness. Open and on display for all to experience. We need this process exemplified in the church. We don't mind letting people know when our feelings are hurt. We will let everyone know when we are mad. We want everyone to know when people fail us or mistreat us. But we don't want anyone to see our vulnerability when we have to admit we treated someone wrongfully or made a mistake concerning a relationship.

People need to witness the process of repentance and forgiveness. This is what happened the night of the baptism. Three people who did not care about the judgment of others. Three people who were so tired of carrying the weight of un-forgiveness and bitterness. We were not going to let this moment pass us by without releasing everything that caused the separation between us.

THE MAN IN THE OFFICE NEXT DOOR repented

openly. I didn't need to hear him repent because I could see it in his eyes. I could feel it in his touch. I had forgiven him before he ever asked. However, his healing demanded his open repentance.

As THE MAN IN THE OFFICE NEXT DOOR looked at my wife and me and asked for us to forgive him, he made a statement that finalized the healing process. He declared that our lives together would be, "As if it never happened!" The moment he made that statement, every weight lifted. There was no longer any place for rejection, no place for inadequacy, resentment, anger, nor any such stronghold.

"As if it never happened," cleaned my heart, spirit, and memory AS IF IT NEVER HAPPENED!

I didn't have to attend a series of counseling sessions nor go through an inner healing course. We did not have to hash out and relive every moment of failure. One statement declared from the heart provided the freedom that we all needed to leave the past in the water and come out as if it never happened.

One of the most remarkable things that happened during the baptism occurred in a moment of spontaneity. As THE MAN IN THE OFFICE NEXT DOOR spoke to my wife and me, I noticed movement out of the corner of my eye. I looked to my right and saw our pastor climbing over the wall of the baptistry.

As he entered the water, you could feel freedom circulating through the atmosphere. The crowd of several hundred were at a fevered pitch of excitement. You could hear screams of victory, sounds of weeping, shouts of joy, and loud sounds of victory filled the whole sanctuary.

Freedom was not only proclaimed to two or three families; dozens of families connected with the liberty filling the room. Hundreds and hundreds of people were experiencing the same victory we were because real humility and honest repentance and forgiveness were prevailing!

As Pastor crawled into the water, he grabbed my arm and the arm of THE MAN IN THE OFFICE NEXT DOOR. He looked at the men assisting with the baptisms and said, "Baptize us all three together."

I cannot articulate the feeling of freedom I was experiencing. Years of intercession were culminating in this moment of unity. Here were the father and his two sons, who were no longer bound by conflict, entering into the most extraordinary event given to display the death of the past and the rise of the future.

We three were about to willingly lie back into a watery grave and submit ourselves to the death of every event and emotion tied to our past together. We knew that we would emerge together, leaving our past confined to the past, and burst forth into newness of life.

THE MAN IN THE OFFICE NEXT DOOR, our pastor, and I laid back into the baptismal waters. All of a sudden, I lost all strength. I went into the water, but I couldn't lift myself out of the water. Thankfully, there was a man who reached his arms under me and lifted me out of the water. I was lifeless. I could feel my body, and I was aware of my surroundings, but I couldn't activate movement within my body. Another gentleman wrapped his arms around me under my shoulders and floated me over to the corner of the pool. I just lay lifeless in the tangible presence of God.

You can debate theology; you can debate doctrine, but you cannot debate the tangible presence of a living God!

As I floated there in the water, I could faintly hear the prayer of intercession being offered over me by the gentleman in whose arms I lay. I began to gain some control of my body again. I opened my eyes and to my left was my pastor, lying lifeless in God's presence just as I was. I worked up enough strength to roll over and embrace him. As I kissed his forehead, he opened his eyes to notice it was me. He looked at me and said, "I love you so much."

These words penetrated to the depths of my heart and spirit. He had told me many times he loved me, but this time those words carried a new emphasis. I knew he was proud of my humility and obedience. You see, I had always longed for the love of a dad in my life. My dad never told me he loved me or that he was proud of me outside of a drunken state of mind. He, being an alcoholic most of his life and all of mine, wasn't much on verbalizing his emotions. To hear these words and know that "my dad" was proud of me was all I needed to complete the healing process that night.

I finally had the strength to stand up. Just as I stood, I saw my wife being floated towards the corner of the baptistry. Here was the love of my life weightless in the presence of the Lord. Emotion hit me again, and all I could do was grasp each side of her face and kiss her forehead. I knew Holy Spirit was performing surgery on her emotions and heart.

I had been married to this woman for almost twenty-four years at this time, so, needless to say, I knew her pretty well. My wife is one of the most loyal people on earth. She loves hard. When she commits her friendship to you, you will have a friend for life. If you know anyone like this, you know the opposite side of the coin, as well. If you misuse their trust or are not loyal to them, they will close you out of their hearts and lives.

This describes my wife perfectly. I knew that she would have to have a real encounter with God for her to experience the repentance and forgiveness being offered that night.

She was experiencing such an encounter. I could see the healing presence of Holy Spirit all over my beautiful wife. I could sense the Lord removing all the anger, hate, and emotional walls she had built up inside her heart. She was floating on a surgeon's bed of water, immersed in the presence of forgiveness. I knew she would come out of the water a new woman.

That she did! It was, "Like it never happened!"

LESSON LEARNED: No matter what the requirement is, it is worth it to obtain peace. God doesn't often show up the same way He did previously. Sometimes our healing comes by prayer, sometimes it comes by fasting and sometimes our healing may only come through other forms of obedience. However, whatever the requirement is, trust me, it is worth it!

John 16:21 says, *"Whenever a woman is in labor she has pain, because her hour has come; but when she gives birth to the child, she no longer remembers the anguish because of the joy that a child has been born into the world."* (NASV)

God spoke to and delivered His people by many different ways. Jesus healed through SO many different means. It doesn't matter if you deliver your promised child in a car, a bathtub, or a hospital! Just keep pressing forward until your promise is alive in your arms!

The Open-Door Policy

Final Thoughts

OFFICE DOOR 1:

The next night was like most any other night. I kissed my wife and children and told them good night. I then went to bed. I usually have no problem falling asleep, and this night was no different. I went to sleep almost immediately. I was still amazed and excited over what had taken place the night before at the revival service.

After being asleep for only twenty-five minutes or so, I woke up. My wife and I both sleep with pillows surrounding us. I like to wrap my legs and arms around my pillows as I sleep on my side. I have a pillow on each side, so there are already pillows waiting for me to grab and continue my rest when I turn over.

Well, when I woke up after a few minutes of being asleep, I was holding one of my pillows, but it was as if the pillow was the Lord. I woke up weeping and saying, "I love you so much, Jesus. Thank you, Jesus. Thank you, Jesus."

Immediately I was given the title of this book, "THE MAN IN THE OFFICE NEXT DOOR."

I heard in my spirit, "I want you and Pastor Marty to write this book together."

It was so real to me that I jumped up and grabbed my computer. For the next hour or so, I wrote the first chapter of this book. Now, this may not seem like a very big deal to you, but I am one of the least likely people to write books. I had not written a book since the early 2000s. I had only written two books my whole life. So, for me to wake up, grab my computer, and write an entire chapter of a book without thought, it had to be the Lord.

The Lord told me how He wanted us to write this book together to show that, at times, our perspective is not the ultimate reality. Sometimes we can get so caught up in our thoughts and feelings that we fail to see what others are thinking or feeling. We become introverted to the point we only care about our perspective of the situation, and we lose the ability to see what is happening.

I did not know how THE MAN IN THE OFFICE NEXT DOOR was feeling about our conflict. I had no point of reference to draw the conclusions he was drawing. He couldn't see the situation through my eyes because my own life experiences stained them.

We can't expect people to think, act, resolve conflict, or do what we would do in any given situation because we are all driven by different life experiences. We each draw from different mental and emotional wells. Sometimes we don't hold the ability to draw the same conclusion as others concerning a particular conflict or situation. It is elementary for us to conclude people should always think as we think about something. It is not rational to expect that our emotional reaction is the correct and only reaction that should be allowed during conflict.

We who fill leadership positions within the church or in the secular arena must be willing to see each conflict from all perspectives. We cannot become selfish and only protect our viewpoint and emotions. I believe leaders have to be strong. I know that leaders have to be wise, seasoned, and able to make hard decisions and stand by their decisions. I get it! However, showing vulnerability at times is not a weakness.

Jesus, Himself, was regularly allowing "unworthy" people to touch Him in ways that were not lawful. Jesus always put Himself in situations where He was questioned, His decisions were in question, and even His motives were questioned. Even in times of rebuke, Jesus understood why they thought the way they did. He saw their perspective, and He didn't react with the state of mind that the people were threatening His Authority. He loved the people, and His goal was to bring truth, understanding, and healing to everyone involved.

We leaders tend to think, if someone challenges our perspective or decision, the person is rebellious. We are so busy chasing "Jezebel spirits" that we push away good loyal people who would give their lives for us though they might disagree or need clarity on a decision we have made.

We must have an open-door policy when it comes to handling conflict and disagreements. An open-door policy comes from the concept of just being open to the people who are friends and confidants in your life. We leaders are to make ourselves available to those under our leadership and/or authority. We can't close the door to protect our hearts and emotions, forgetting that we are called to protect those who are doing life with us.

The world doesn't need superheroes, especially in the church. We need men and women who are confident, having integrity and strong character to lead God's people. These men and women also have to be willing to admit when they are wrong. They have to be ready to make things right between themselves and others, no matter the cost.

I wrote my perspective of the events described in this book to inspire you never to let conflict become unforgiveness. Never let a disagreement go unresolved to the point that anger, hate, and separation filtrate into your life and relationships. Whatever you have to do to offer the opportunity for repentance and forgiveness, DO IT!

Don't let another second go by! Pick up the phone, write an email, send a text, do something right now to begin the healing process!

OFFICE DOOR 2:

While serving in youth ministry at a small church in Cumming, Georgia, from 2001-2006, I felt the prompting of the Lord to write a book. I had never written a book in my life. Because I don't like to read, I didn't even know where to start. English Literature was one of my worst subjects all through school.

How can someone possibly write a book when he doesn't even read books?

For a year or so, I put notes on paper and even taught in my youth ministry the material I wanted to use in the book. It just never manifested in book form. Then a decade or so later, I felt the nudge to write two or three more books. I had the titles and the main points I wanted to cover in the books and stories to add to them. I just could not make myself write them. I would continuously add to my notes for the books. I just could not seem to make it happen in book form.

Years would pass. No books. No books until THE MAN IN THE OFFICE NEXT DOOR approached me one evening and said the Lord had given him a dream or a vision to write a book about our experiences over the past six years. He shared the book title and how he thought it should be laid out. He said he would relate his feelings and his side of the story, and then I would share my feelings and my side of the story. He told me about how the Lord woke him up one night and gave him the dream for writing the book and that he had written quite a bit of it already.

It was a great idea, in theory. The problem was, I don't write. I have great ideas and intentions, but I don't write. That is, until now.

I love the fact that God can take situations and circumstances and perspectives from two completely different individuals and, at some point, allow them to bring those issues to Him so He can project them through His lens.

You see, the lens through which I see things is blurry at times. My lens had gotten dirty from past hurts and rejection, cracked from past issues that went unconfronted, and, therefore, went unresolved. It had become stained with setback after setback in past relationships.

When I would get hurt in a relationship, I would carry

that hurt into the next relationship and then see that next person the way I saw the last person. If "they" offended me, it wouldn't be long until the "next one" offended me. My lens saw it this way: If "they" offended me, it won't be long until the "next one" offends me. If "they" betrayed me, it won't be long until the "next one" betrays me. If "they" let me down, it won't be long until the "next one" lets me down.

Looking through this type of lens always leads to being halfway in these types of relationships. When you don't go into a relationship with total commitment, at some point, you begin to look for a way of escape. The easiest way to escape is to magnify what "they" did, then blame "them" for it, and slowly withdraw from them.

That type of disconnect isn't healthy for any relationship and typically causes a relationship to end prematurely while using that stained lens to look for another relationship. It isn't fair at all for those who surround you. But it is far easier to blame "the next one" than it is to own your faults and clean the lens.

The lens-cleaning moment for me was life-changing. I see others in a different light now. I don't feel like everyone's out to get me. I traded in my victim mentality for a victorious mentality. I am super quick to repent and super quick to forgive these days. Why? My lens has been cleaned.

I watched God take a hopeless situation and make it LIKE IT NEVER HAPPENED! I quickly realized unforgiveness had chained me to my PAST; it poisoned my PRESENT, and it would have hindered me from what the Lord had for my FUTURE.

To forgive meant I had to choose to set a prisoner

free. As I did, I realized that prisoner was me!

One of the most important things the Lord spoke to me through this entire six years of silence in our relationship was this: Believing I had a right to hold a grudge didn't make it right!

Listen, friend, if you read this entire book from cover to cover, and it has hit close to home with you, meaning that you can think of a person or maybe a few people you haven't spoken to due to unresolved conflict, do me a favor. Pray. Ask the Lord this one question: "Who is my 'MAN IN THE OFFICE NEXT DOOR'?" Who do I have aught against? Who offended me? Who am I bitter towards? Who causes me to cringe when they walk into the room?

Then, ask the Lord to give you the strength and words to say and then reach out to that one. Life is too short not to. Don't allow the enemy to rob you of six years, or more, of your life, as I did.

You'll never get AHEAD as long as you're always trying to get EVEN!

Make the phone call, send the email, or shoot a text to the person.

But first, repent.

Looking back on our six-year struggle, I can see where I was in error. The Lord opened my eyes to show me moments where I had malice in my heart. The Spirit of God began to walk me back in time over the past six years to show me the moments when MY heart wasn't right toward THE MAN IN THE OFFICE NEXT DOOR. And many times, when YOUR own heart isn't right, you can't rightfully receive what comes from the hearts of those closest to you.

I came to realize it wasn't all him. I acted immaturely many times. I was self-absorbed and emotional, not to mention irrational. If I am honest, I was jealous and envious. My heart was cold most of the time when I was around him. That was on me. Not him.

The more I allowed myself to get offended with something he did or said, the more anger would rise within me. The angrier I got, the worse our relationship got. I should have communicated my feelings more. I should have talked through and processed my emotions with him. By not doing that, I continued to just "scratch the itch" and not treat it appropriately.

It's like the time I got poison oak on my shoulders while working outdoors one day. When I got home that evening, I began to lean back against the doorframes in my home to scratch between my shoulders in hopes of relieving the nagging itch. What felt good for a moment quickly began to agitate the poison oak all the more. Minutes later, I found myself rolling around on my back on my bedroom carpet, scratching again. That resulted in spreading the poison oak that was around my shoulder blade area to my entire back.

Unresolved, "untreated" conflict feels good when you're able to scratch it. I scratched the itch of unresolved conflict by coming home and sharing it with my wife. Then my kids would overhear us discussing it, and I would then have to explain some things. Every time I shared something with one of my youth leaders or our support staff members, it was a relief to me, like I was able to "scratch the itch." But eventually, ultimately, that stuff spread like the poison it was.

Proverbs 15:18 says, *"A hot-tempered person stirs up conflict, but the one who is patient calms a quarrel."*

I was that hot-tempered person. I was the one stirring up conflict. It was as if I was trying to convince others how wrong HE was. And it felt good to talk to others about him. But, I should have been talking to him.

So, I urge you to hit conflict head-on. Deal with it quickly. Don't let it go unresolved. Be quick to admit your faults. Repent of wrongdoing on your part and allow the Lord to turn your heart first. I promise, once you turn your heart to the Father, He can turn "their" heart to yours.

One final note: the man I've referred to as THE MAN IN THE OFFICE NEXT DOOR is now one of my very best friends. We talk frequently. We respect and honor each other.

His name is David Edmondson. He is the pastor of a thriving church in Flowery Branch, Georgia.

David, I love, admire, and honor you, sir. I blew it the first time. But, I'll spend the rest of my life serving alongside you, not behind four walls and a roof, but in life. It's an honor for me to stand beside you from this day forward as your MAN IN THE OFFICE NEXT DOOR.

LIKE IT NEVER HAPPENED!

The "Bystanders"

Collateral Damage

Divisions between people in the Body of Christ do not happen in a vacuum. "Bystanders" always suffer when people decide to disregard the clear teaching of Jesus to forgive. In this case, the men in the offices next door to each other have had their say. They have confessed to the bad and acknowledged the good that the Holy Spirit has salvaged from their division.

We thought it instructive to also give voice to some of the people near the epicenter of the divide documented in this book, to show how others can be hurt and offended by the rash actions of leaders who might otherwise think their actions only affect themselves.

TODD SMITH

Words cannot adequately describe the deep pain I experienced due to Pastor David and Pastor Marty's division. Like any father, my heart bled for both my son's in the Lord. I watched at a distance as my soul grieved for both of them. I invited Pastor David to speak at the North Georgia Revival for two reasons: one, I knew he could deliver a "now" word to the people in attendance. Secondly, in my spirit, I was hoping this could be the beginning of their reconciliation. I knew they could not remain in the glorious atmosphere of revival and not experience reconciliation.

After Pastor David preached, not much changed, so I took it to the next level; I invited Pastor David to join Pastor Marty in the water to help baptize those seeking an encounter with God. That was the beginning of a miracle.

One of the greatest nights of my life was when I joined the two of them in the baptismal waters at the North Georgia Revival. The three of us were baptized simultaneously, and the Holy Spirit came and ignited a more profound and greater fire in each of us. I could not be more proud of these two great men who humbled themselves before the world, and God has taken them and the revival to the next level.

I love you both!

KAREN SMITH

I consider one of the greatest callings - if not *the* greatest calling in my life - is that of a mother. Todd and I have two wonderful sons, Ty and Ethan. They are proof that Jesus loves me because each of them is such a gift from Him! I often tell people that Todd and I really have four sons: two natural sons and two sons in the Lord.

Pastor David and Pastor Marty have been a part of our lives for over twenty years. And yes, I call them both "Pastor" out of great respect for them even though I consider them sons in the Lord. Pastor Marty was saved under our ministry in 1995, and Pastor David came into our lives not long after. They have loved and respected Todd and me as long as we have known them. There are no two finer men on the earth.

When division came into their lives, and their relationship was severed, my heart was crushed. Like any good mom would, I decided to position myself to stay right "in the middle." I refused to choose sides, no matter who I thought was right or wrong. My heart loved them both. I kept my peace as I prayed for them both. I determined to remain steady and immovable as I waited on reconciliation. I knew a reunion between them would one day come because of the caliber of men they both are and the presence of God that rests on them.

Then the night came in what I still consider the most outstanding church service I have ever experienced in my life. Pastor David preached an unbelievable message during the revival at Christ Fellowship Church. As he concluded, he called for Pastor Marty to come to the stage. The two and their families reunited in the most powerful display of forgiveness I have ever seen!

During those years of separation, I knew Pastor David and Pastor Marty didn't need my opinion or advice. What they needed from me was support and the knowledge that my heart for both of them had not changed.

Sometimes with your children, you've got to know when to be quiet and just love them. You watch them walk through situations, and you love them. You watch them make decisions, and you love them. You watch them make choices, and you love them. And that's what I did. I loved them as they struggled in those years, and I love them today, just like it never happened! My love for them will never change.

PAULA DARRACOTT:

It was Valentine's Day, 2013; I woke up and set out gifts for Madison and Carson like every Valentine's Day since they were born. I drove to work. The sun was shining, I had my heart-covered socks on (I love holiday socks).

I was planning dinner for Marty and the girls. It was going to be a day filled with lots of fun, love, and cupcakes. Marty surprised me when he stopped by my office just before my lunch break with a handful of roses. Little did I know that my real surprise that day would come as he began to tell me that he had been "let go" of his position at the church we had been a part of for the last six years; the church I loved, the youth group I was so very proud of, the people that I considered family. I had laughed with them, cried with them, and I was shocked. Pastor David Edmondson had decided that it was time for us to no longer be on staff with him and Stephanie at Covenant Connections Church.

It made absolutely no sense to me. I had trusted them with our family. Instantly, my trust was destroyed. I felt every negative emotion I could handle. Then it reality hit me. It was at that moment that I needed to "suck it up, buttercup." I had Valentine's dinner to plan. We could not tell our girls because the news would wreck them. We picked up the cupcakes covered with red and pink icing and lots of extra sprinkles and headed to one of our favorite restaurants. Heads up, smiles on!

At dinner, we received a much-needed return phone call from our mentor, coach, and mom, Jeanne Mayo. Marty spoke with her first, and then, as I stepped out of the restaurant to talk to her, I began to fall apart. She, being the best, gave me some excellent advice. She said, "it is all going to be OK. You are ALWAYS in God's hands. You are going to want to defend yourself and Marty, but don't. Don't send an email. Don't send a text. Don't post anything on social media, and don't you dare go get a haircut." Ha! She knew exactly what to say to settle me. I trusted her.

I wiped my eyes, put my smile back on, and finished dinner with my favorite people.

When we got home that night, it felt like hours before the girls were finally off to their rooms and asleep.

Finally, I could talk to Marty about what had just happened. Once I was free to feel, I could not stop crying. I was mad, mad, mad. I was scared, scared, scared. He held me and promised me that we would be just fine. I believed him. He was determined for us not to feel the loss more than we had to. He is the strongest and hardest-working person I know. I trusted him.

The next morning, Marty and I were able to sit across from the table with our pastors, Todd and Karen Smith. These two have been a huge part of our lives since the day we were saved. We could not imagine a life without them. They comforted us and spent time encouraging the gifts that they had always recognized in us. They told us to keep looking forward, not back. Pastor Karen held my hand that day, shed some tears with me, and promised me that "nothing takes God by surprise." I trusted her. Those words brought life to me, and I held on to them.

Somehow, one day turned into weeks that turned into months and then turned into years. Many times I felt caged, silenced, and angry. If I could just tell my story, my side, share my frustrations, my disappointment in both people, and the church, I would feel better. It didn't work.

We never took a break from ministry. We kept loving people, loving God, and serving the new church He had placed us in, Christ Fellowship Church Dawsonville. Our family fell in love with our new church. It took a little time, but the girls finally felt home, and so did we.

Then, February 2018 happened at Christ Fellowship. Our church began to experience a genuine revival. It felt so real, so raw, so different than church had felt in a while. There was a night when Bishop Lance Johnson had preached on unforgiveness and things that you just could not let go of. Well, guess whose face came to my mind. Yes, David Edmondson's. I tried to talk God into believing that I had already dealt with that. He convinced me I was wrong. I was still carrying such angst and resentment and anger and rejection, and the list goes on. So, I did what any strong God-fearing woman would do. I argued with Him as though I would win.

Thankfully, He never let up, and I surrendered this heartbreak to Jesus, the One who loves me most. He promised me that night that He would take this from me and restore love in my heart and restore a very broken relationship. I trusted Him. He had never let me down.

I should have put a time limit on God. He was taking

way too long. Pastor David would preach at our church. He would leave, and nothing had changed. You see, if I had been in charge, I would have just tossed Marty and David in a room together, locked the door, and told them not to come out until they were hugging. We all know that probably would not have ended well.

God had a better plan. He initiated the most humbling, genuine moment of forgiveness I have ever witnessed at an altar and in the baptismal waters at Christ Fellowship Church. In one moment, it was done. God has kept His promise to me. We hugged, we cried, we forgave, we loved, and we became family again. I trusted them.

Trust is such a powerful thing, yet it never comes easy. Trust simply means the belief in the reliability, truth, ability, or strength in someone or something. On this day, what was broken was mended, and trust was restored!

STEPHANIE EDMONDSON:

When we were little, I'm pretty sure Marty was my favorite cousin. We were the closest in age. As young kids, our families were always together at Granny Sugars and PawPaw Charles' house. Then we all grew up.

I remember being so excited for Marty and Paula to be our youth pastors. We called our staff "the dream team." As time went on, things got ugly - uglier than you can imagine. Marty and I would pass each other in the church, and worse than not even speaking, we wouldn't even look at each other.

There was division among the staff. And there was division in the church.

In February 2013, Marty was dismissed from the church. Things got even worse after that. Lies and rumors were rampant, and we heard them all. It was a long six years filled with hate and anger toward part of my family.

And then there was the night of January 13, 2019, a night of refreshing, a night of forgiveness, restoration, and healing. I am so thankful for this night.

I am so thankful that I have a husband that is a man after God's heart. He hears from the Lord and is a man of forgiveness and obedience. I love you, David Edmondson. You are a good man.

REAGAN EDMONDSON:

This experience was very hard on my family and me. I never really understood everything that was happening because I was so young at the time. All I knew was that I was losing a part of my family that meant everything to me.

Ever since the day Uncle Marty, Aunt Paula, and my cousins left the church, things never felt the same. I was so used to seeing my family not only at church but outside church, as well. This whole misunderstanding changed our lives tremendously.

When I was younger, we would always get together with the Darracotts, and before I knew it, it was all over. I didn't get to grow up and be close with my cousins and the rest of my family like I wished. I never got to spend another Thanksgiving, Christmas,

Halloween, or any holiday with them. Noah, Madison, Carson, and I never got to have sleepovers ever again. Family has always been very important for me. It was terrible growing up with part of my family disliking me and barely knowing me. It was tough to see that side of the family getting together and our not being invited. It always confused me because my parents would talk about "forgiveness" as a huge part of Christian lives, but they never forgave each other.

The night that our family was restored, I felt so much heartache go away. I knew when my dad asked for Uncle Marty that something was going to happen. When we were all called on stage, I specifically remember Uncle Marty saying to me, "I will make it up to you," which made me break down in tears.

I am beyond blessed that our family is whole again. I love you so much, Uncle Marty, Aunt Paula, Madison, and Carson.

Like It Never Happened.

MADISON DARRACOTT:

Being family, I felt the immediate effects of everything that went down in February of 2013. I was too young for them to tell me every detail of what happened but old enough to fill in the blanks on my own. I was heartbroken, and my emotions were all over the place. Sad, mad, bitter, then sad again.

In an instant, two of my closest cousins weren't a part of my life anymore. My Aunt Step & Uncle David had become strangers to me. No more sleepovers, no more after church lunches, no more holidays together. We stopped following each other on

Instagram; we unfriended each other on Facebook. From one-hundred to zero. Like we never even knew each other.

Then revival happened, and they started coming to Sunday night services more often than not. And I hated every second of it. It hurt me to be in the same room as them. It hurt too bad to see their faces again. The night that everything (the restoration) happened, January 13, 2019, I missed all of Uncle David's sermon. I wasn't feeling great and, to be honest, didn't want to sit in a service listening to him speak, so after I got done leading worship, I looked at Jhoana and asked her if she'd leave with me. So we did. We left the church building and went to grab something in a drive-thru.

When we returned, we could hear Uncle David closing his message on the TV in the lobby. I heard him call for my dad, and I took off running to the sanctuary. You know what happened next: full restoration, complete healing, such forgiveness.

Rea, Noah, Aunt Step, Uncle David, I love you guys so much.

Like. It. Never. Happened.

NOAH EDMONDSON:

It was 2013, the single worst year of my entire life. My cousins, my family, divided for what seemed like would be forever.

Until then, we had the closest family relationship you could ever know: Thanksgiving dinners, Christmas Eve morning playing football at Granny Sugar's house, spend-the-night parties, just a close family bond that we all had with my cousins and Uncle Marty and Aunt Paula. Many, many good memories we shared.

In 2013, I remember seeing a picture through social media of all of the family at Thanksgiving, except us. This hurt me to my core. Why weren't we invited? Why were we left out? One day, I found out that they were leaving the church for reasons that I didn't even know about. I had no idea that anything was going on. I didn't understand why they would leave just out of plain sight in the middle of our lives.

Through some snooping in on my parents, I found out that some drama was happening behind the scenes that I couldn't know about. As the days went on, we still shared contact, texts off and on. That became weeks, months, and turned into years of no contact with each other. I once asked my dad, "How come we haven't seen the family in a while?" But I got little to no response. I knew they were going to church in Dawsonville now, and that's all that I knew. I had so many questions about the world, I would see families posting pictures on social media, all together, and it would make me feel so alone and so angry. Why couldn't we have that? Why was it like this now after all the good times we all had together?

I would question God mostly because they are both pastors; this isn't something that happens in the church. Why is it happening to us?

Almost six years passed with no contact at all. Then on January 13, 2019, our lives would change forever. I just had an odd feeling that Sunday afternoon, "I need to go to church." I didn't know why, but something just kept telling me to go to the revival and see what it's all about. I saw Carson, Madison, Uncle Marty, and Aunt Paula but didn't know how to say hello or greet family that I hadn't talked to in almost six years.

We got to the end of the service, and my dad was wrapping up his sermon. Then he called Uncle Marty to the stage, and I was thinking to myself and looked at my sister, "Wait, what"? Why would he call him up? He began to start apologizing to him.

"There's no way this is happening!" I thought I was in a dream, and then he called up both of our families. I had never had a complete breakdown like when I looked into my cousins' eyes that I haven't spoken to or seen in years.

I looked at Uncle Marty, with his arms held out wide, and all that I could get out is, "I missed you so much, Man!"

It was complete forgiveness, restoration. We were a family again. It was one of the most incredible days of my entire life, and I will never again question God's plan for our lives.

REBECCA LEAPHART:

Both of these men and their wives impacted and imparted into my life in their own unique and necessary ways. It was extremely painful to feel the need to keep that separate.

I was a part of the church staff as a whole and a very involved youth leader. I saw much of the conflict first-hand. It was always the elephant in the room, from meetings to fellowships, to church service itself. If you knew, you felt the tension.

Sometimes it was trivial, like not knowing where to sit at football games if both families were there. Other times, it seemed much more significant, like choosing to step down from a youth ministry I loved because the pressure between the two was exhausting. So many choices were made to avoid adding to the tension. Lines were invisibly and silently drawn, but you knew you had to choose. Many years and many big life moments were missed.

Upon their reconciliation, I was just so proud and so thankful. Their repentance trumped everything else. I can only imagine both the courage and humility it took for this to happen. It was like the heaviness in the air we had all experienced for years finally lifted. A breath of fresh air entered, and invisible walls shattered. Tensions released.

The reconciliation also reconciled many of their leaders to one another. Friendships restored. So much heartache was mended in a matter of moments. I'm so thankful we can all be in the same room, smile, laugh, hug, share life, and minister together. You get used to living a certain way and molding your habits and choices around division, but when that is no longer an option, you are free from chains you didn't even know bound you.

JOEL FLORES:

We all worked at the church, and things seemed all right, but every once in a while, one or the other would tell me something that wouldn't sit well with me Nothing too wrong, just "pick me" type situations.

As months passed by, tensions got stronger, and we felt the division. There was no peace. Our staff lunches were no longer. It made me sad because it felt like the church family was unbelievers. We were the leaders! And we were suffering.

My spiritual dad and my favorite funny uncle were not talking. I didn't know what to do or how to feel. It was like, Why can't we move past this? Let's make up! We're family! We love each other! Who do I pick?

I spent time with both separately, of course. I looked up to them; they were both cool! They are both the best senior and youth pastor in the world! And they were the best of friends to me. I worked out with Pastor Marty, and I hunted with Pastor David.

Years went by, and we all separated. Pastor Marty went to Dawsonville, and we stayed in Flowery Branch. I remembered we went to Pastor Marty's church for a conference about two years ago. I was standing in the back, and Pastor Marty came to me and spoke words of encouragement, and it surprised me. He hadn't spoken to me in years. At that moment, I felt the shift; I felt a change was coming. Pastor Marty's heart was softened, and he was ready.

JENNIFER BROWNING & FAMILY:

Covenant Connections Church was my safe place & reGeneration Youth had become a safe place for my boys. In 2013, all that changed.

As a parent, I had to make one of the hardest decisions I would ever make. As a single mom and the head of my household, I put my emotions aside and did what was right for my boys. After many days of prayer and fasting, I chose to leave the only church family my boys and I had ever known and loved.

Pastors David and Stephanie had been my family since moving to Georgia in 2001. God had spoken to me clearly, and obedience was my only option. I knew God's voice, and I was at complete peace. Jordan, Justin, and Jason all had a very close relationship with Pastor Marty, Paula, and their family.

It was hard for our family, but walking along the journey with the Darracott family and trying to understand the WHY of this whole situation was even more challenging. The anger, bitterness, and hurt we felt was not even close to what they experienced. The constant struggle within me was with the loss of a very special friendship.

We made the transition to Christ Fellowship Church, our new church home. The boys had a wonderful middle school and high school experience with incredible youth leaders over the years. I will forever be grateful for Pastor Marty and Mrs. Paula. They always spoke life into them and wanted the best for them.

Everything changed when revival started. We all went through different stages of repentance as the Lord worked on each of us individually and as a corporate church. We all felt something was about to shift, but we did not know when, where, or what. We did know God was up to something. The atmosphere was weighted and hard to explain.

In January 2019, as Pastor David and Pastor Marty stood before our church in total surrender and forgiveness, everything changed. That night all the hurt, bitterness, and anger turned into love and forgiveness. God stepped in and changed everyone in the room.

I will never be the same, and I look at all my relationships differently and try to see them through His eyes.

Grateful & Thankful. Like it Never Happened!!

JERRY LEAPHART:

I sat in my office one afternoon and heard the whole transaction. After years of tension and turmoil, deep lines drawn, and sides taken, voices were raised, doors were slammed, and all at once, Pastor Marty was leaving, and Pastor David was hardened.

I watched as Pastor Marty hugged other staff members good-bye, and I hoped for the same. I went in for a hug, and he shook his head and turned to get in his car. As I watched him drive away, I felt like I had failed these men.

In a moment, covenants were broken, and years of friendships were lost. I felt stuck in the middle of two great mountains - confused at how and why this was happening and why I felt like I had to keep it all together.

Why couldn't these men work out their issues? Why couldn't they be professional? Why did I have to choose?

As a young minister, I had gleaned from the wisdom and guidance of Pastor David and Pastor Marty. All I had ever known in ministry were these two men's extraordinary leadership. I worked each day alongside them in the same office for several years as that awful tension mounted.

There was a great void in the years that followed that afternoon. We went our separate ways, and no one spoke of the great split unless it was how someone was treating someone else unfairly or in a manner they didn't like. As an intercessor, all I could do was pray.

The turmoil and weight were great. However, I didn't know how great until January 13, 2019. When it happened, I felt years of release and endless nights of intercession justified. I wept for days, tears of release and thankfulness.

I never thought I would be writing about this. And honestly, it is like it never happened.

CARSON DARRACOTT:

I was young when it all happened. All I knew was my dad was the youth pastor one day, and then the next, he wasn't. I didn't know exactly why at the time; I just knew that Dad being released meant I wouldn't see my family much anymore, if I even got to at all.

We were always together. There were countless sleepovers, after-church lunches, and family gatherings that we would do with each other. So obviously, it was a drastic change in 2013 to go from seeing each other nearly every day to not seeing each other at all. I was twelve at the time, so it was hard to fully grasp what had happened, but I think people underestimate how much a twelve-year-old can understand.

I felt all the emotions; anger, sadness, bitterness, and frustration. As I grew up and continued to find out more about the story, those emotions stayed with me. It became comfortable to have a hardened side of myself toward the people who hurt my family.

The first time I heard that Pastor David was going to be preaching at the revival, all that rage and whirl of emotion told me not to go. Why would I sit in a service under someone who hurt me so badly? I went reluctantly because, if my dad could sit in that service under him, so could I. He came again and again, but it never got more comfortable to see him, Stephanie, Reagan, and Noah.

Then January 13, 2019, happened. I was taking pictures when I heard him call for my dad. I immediately knew what was about to happen, and I couldn't stop shaking and could barely even stand. You know what happened next. That was the first time in nearly seven years that I was able to hug my aunt and uncle, and the first time I was able to embrace Noah and Reagan without hidden pain. I've never been so thankful. Uncle David, Aunt Steph, Noah, and Reagan, I love y'all so much!

Made in the USA
Coppell, TX
05 January 2022